POLICY STUDIES IN EMPLOYMENT AND WELFARE NUMBER 13

General Editors: Sar A. Levitan and Garth L. Mangum

Work and Welfare Go Together

Sar A. Levitan
Martin Rein
David Marwick

The Johns Hopkins University Press, Baltimore and London

The Johns Hopkins University Press, Baltimore, Maryland 21218
The Johns Hopkins University Press Ltd., London

Library of Congress Catalog Card Number 72-3227
International Standard Book Number 0-8018-1420-0 (clothbound edition)
International Standard Book Number 0-8018-1421-9 (paperbound edition)

Originally published, 1972
Paperback edition, 1972

This study was prepared under a grant from The Ford Foundation.

A Joint Publication of the Center for Manpower Policy Studies of The George Washington University, and the Joint Center for Urban Studies of Harvard University and the Massachusetts Institute of Technology.

Graphics by *The Hatchet*, Washington, D.C.

Library of Congress Cataloging in Publication data will be found on the last printed page of this book.

Contents

Tables

Charts

Preface

Given the rising affluence of the American people and the secular decline of poverty, the goal of eliminating poverty in the United States by the second centennial of the nation appears feasible. To raise the 25 million poor to the poverty threshold as defined by government criteria would require only about one percent of the national income.

The challenge of eradicating poverty is, however, much more complicated than transferring an additional $10 billion. The challenge of a viable welfare system is to provide adequately for those who cannot help themselves, retain incentives for the able-bodied to contribute to their own support, and keep the level of costs acceptable to the majority who foot the bill.

The present welfare system misses each of these three marks. Assistance provided is normally far below the poverty threshold, incentives for work are inadequate, and even the minimal levels of support are given grudgingly. Nonetheless, the network of public assistance programs has spread, at ever increasing costs. Seven of every hundred people in the United States are now on welfare, at an annual cost of $19 billion.

The enormous growth of public assistance during the last decade has encouraged schemes to substitute workfare for welfare, to transmute relief recipients into taxpayers. Work and welfare have typically been portrayed as substitutes, but for an increasingly large proportion of the population the choice is not work *or* welfare but work *and* welfare. A series of programs to reform the welfare system and its recipients has evolved during the administrations of Presidents Kennedy, Johnson, and Nixon, justified alternately as restoring relief recipients to economic independence and protecting taxpayers and the fabric of society. Consideration of far more massive efforts has included administration proposals and considerable congressional hearings and debate. While the numerous proposals vary widely in philosophy and mechanics, an unmistakable theme is the continued and increasing interdependence of work and welfare.

This volume surveys the factors that have contributed to the growth of "welfare" in the United States and examines the components of the welfare system. Present efforts for self-support and government programs designed to improve the earnings of relief recipients are evaluated as a background for the options available in developing a welfare system that encourages recipients to supplement their incomes, even though they may not achieve complete self-support.

This study was prepared under a grant from The Ford Foundation to The George Washington University's Center for Manpower Policy Studies. In accordance with the Foundation's practice, complete responsibility for preparation of the volume was left to the authors.

Work and Welfare Go Together

1

AFDC Today and How It Got There

WELFARE TODAY

The U.S. welfare system has been attacked by its recipients as too niggardly and demeaning and by other critics as an insidious boondoggle. Those who pay have never viewed welfare kindly, but the immediate cause of the present criticism is its increased rate of growth.

Seven of every hundred Americans received federally aided public assistance in late 1971. Expenditures had reached an annual rate of over $19 billion, including almost $10 billion in cash payments to almost 14 million recipients and nearly as much in in-kind benefits. In addition, one million persons received almost $800 million in state and locally financed general assistance. The federally aided public assistance system included four categorical programs: Old Age Assistance, Aid to the Blind, Aid to the Permanently and Totally Disabled, and Aid to Families with Dependent Children (AFDC). The last of these programs is by far the largest and has become virtually synonymous with the term "welfare" (Chart 1). In addition, nonservice-connected pensions paid to 2.8

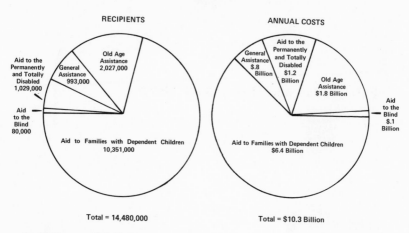

CHART 1. WHO GETS PUBLIC ASSISTANCE AND HOW MUCH?
(as of September 1971)

RECIPIENTS

ANNUAL COSTS

Aid to the Permanently and Totally Disabled 1,029,000

General Assistance 993,000

Old Age Assistance 2,027,000

Aid to the Blind 80,000

Aid to Families with Dependent Children 10,351,000

General Assistance $.8 Billion

Aid to the Permanently and Totally Disabled $1.2 Billion

Old Age Assistance $1.8 Billion

Aid to the Blind $.1 Billion

Aid to Families with Dependent Children $6.4 Billion

Total = 14,480,000

Total = $10.3 Billion

Source: U.S. Department of Health, Education, and Welfare

million needy veterans and their survivors required another $2.3 billion of federal outlays during 1970.

Although the federal government provides more than half of total outlays, AFDC varies considerably from state to state. Average actual payments per family in late 1971 were distributed as follows:

$275 or more	2 states
$225 to $274	10 states
$175 to $224	14 states
$125 to $174	9 states
$ 75 to $124	14 states
Less than $75	2 states

A full accounting of the benefits to recipients of AFDC must include also assistance provided by food stamps, Medicaid, public housing, and social services. In Chicago, for example, a female family head with three children and no earn-

2

ings can receive, in addition to cash payments, food stamps worth $408 annually, full payme⌁ ⌁ ⌁r her medical needs worth an average of $910, and perhaps public housing, though this is available to only a small portion of AFDC families (Table 1).

Table 1. Benefits potentially available to a four-person, female-headed family in Chicago, 1971

| | | Taxes | | | | | |
| | | | Social | Food | Medic- | | Public |
Earnings[a]	AFDC	Income	security	stamps	aid[b]	TOTAL	housing[c]
None	$3,384	—	—	$408	$910	$4,702	$1,416
$1,000	3,384	—	$ 52	288	910	5,530	1,269
2,000	2,890	—	104	288	910	5,984	1,089
3,000	2,224	—	156	288	910	6,266	908
4,000	1,557	—	208	288	910	6,547	728
5,000	890	$164	260	288	910	6,664	547
6,000	224	349	312	288	910	6,761	367
7,000	—	545	364	—	—	6,091	186
8,000	—	723	416	—	—	6,661	6
9,000	—	908	468	—	—	7,624	—

[a]According to the U.S. Bureau of Labor Statistics, fringe benefits may add significantly to the value of work, from $350 at $3,000 annual earnings to $3,600 at $9,000.

[b]Medical vendor payments (Medicaid) are not available to families in cash, since such payments are made on behalf of families with medical needs only. Medicaid benefit represents average payment on behalf of all AFDC families in Illinois. Individual families may receive higher or lower value depending upon medical needs.

[c]Available to only 18 percent of AFDC families in Chicago.

SOURCE: U.S. Department of Health, Education, and Welfare.

The measurable value of belonging to the public assistance system for a family of four with no other income in Chicago, for example, is equal to an income received from full-time work at an hourly wage of $2.30. The addition of public housing to those who qualify is worth another 70 cents. Allowances for work expenses and payroll deductions probably raise the equivalent wage rates by another 25 or 50 cents. Such levels hardly constitute opulence, but they do compare favorably with the earnings of many full-time workers in Chicago.

Nor is Illinois atypical. A dozen states have higher standards of assistance. The same female-headed, four-person family with no earnings could receive—in cash payments, food stamp or surplus commodities, and Medicaid benefits—about $4,938 in New York City, $3,187 in Wilmington, Delaware, and $2,437 in Phoenix, Arizona. Some families also receive a public housing bonus worth several hundred dollars a year.[1] However, actual payments frequently fall short of amounts available under federal and state laws.

ROOTS OF THE PRESENT PROGRAM

"Decent provision for the poor," Samuel Johnson observed, "is the time test of civilization." Even though the Bible is not optimistic about the disappearance of poverty, it commanded "thou shalt open thine hand wide unto thy brother, to thy poor, and to thy needy, in thy land" [Deuteronomy XV: 11].

American programs are based on English law dating as far back as the fourteenth century. This first Law of Settlement in 1388, the Elizabethan Poor Law of 1601, and the Poor Law Report of 1834 established guidelines which are hauntingly familiar. Central was the distinction between the employable and unemployable. The former were considered unworthy of assistance; the latter were considered "deserving," and various modes of help were used, but aid was kept less desirable than potential earnings. Schemes to require the poor to work in exchange for assistance met scant success. Assistance was provided locally, in part to discourage mobility. Finally, the adequacy and availability of aid was cyclical, with periods of leniency—frequently in response to economic crises—followed by reaction and restrictiveness.[2]

A variety of institutional arrangements was used in this country, with varying participation by private eleemosynary groups. Constant, however, was the belief that the poor were to blame for their condition.

American income maintenance programs began to take their present shape during the two decades preceding World War I, a period marked by great ferment and pressure for social reform. State provisions for widows and orphans were consistent with the premium traditionally placed on family cohesiveness. The level of aid varied widely, but remained low even in the prosperous twenties. By 1926 all but six states had mothers' aid programs; by 1933 old age assistance was compulsory in twenty-five states. Although state efforts were obviously gaining momentum, the expanding aid offered by private, local, and state programs was completely overwhelmed by the Great Depression. The worst economic catastrophe in modern history called for a variety of measures to provide income.

Faced with critical mass unemployment and the need to provide income during the depression of the 1930s, the architects of the New Deal opted for job creation rather than outright relief. To help people who could not find work in the marketplace, the federal government assumed, within budgetary constraints, the responsibility as the "employer of last resort." Efforts in this vein were abandoned as World War II brought full employment.

The New Deal legislation designed two distinct cash support programs which have survived to the present and expanded manifoldly. Enacted under the Social Security Act of 1935, these programs were the federal government's first sustained involvement in general income maintenance. First, two contributory social insurance programs—unemployment insurance and old-age insurance—distribute income payments on the basis of prior earnings and tax contributions. With coverage extended to survivors and the disabled, and health insurance also added, the original program of Old Age Insurance became Old Age, Survivors, Disability, and Health Insurance (OASDHI)—commonly called "social security." Because benefits under the social insurance programs depend on prior earnings and labor force attachment, only those with income in the past qualify for future payments. The second set of programs provides assistance on the basis of need alone. The public assistance components were originally intended as transitional, providing assistance until the social security system encompassed them. However, the expectation that public assistance would wither away was not realized. An increasing number of the elderly receive both social security and welfare; the long-term unemployed can, in some cases, benefit from unemployment insurance and then public assistance; social insurance offers little assistance to unmarried, separated, or divorced female heads of families, but is more generous to those whose needs are due to catastrophic circumstances, such as the death or disability of the spouse. From its inception, AFDC has grown rapidly and almost without interruption. It continues the dichotomy between, on the one hand, those who had worked and who would be helped during brief periods of unemployment or after they were no longer able to work and, on the other, those who had little expectation of self-support.

GROWTH OF AFDC

The AFDC program has grown enormously in thirty-five years and recently has expanded at an accelerating rate. In each decade between 1936 and 1966, the number of recipients approximately doubled; the next doubling occurred within four years (Chart 2).

The rise of AFDC during the 1960s seems not at all congruent with other trends of the past decade. Between 1960 and 1969 the number of Americans below the poverty level dropped steadily from 40 million to 24 million, or from 22 percent of the population to 12 percent; the unemployment rate, after a spurt up to 6.7 percent in 1961, fell below 4 percent in 1965 and stayed at that level until the end of the decade. But the AFDC rolls rose from 2.9 million at the beginning of 1960 to 7.3 million at the end of 1969, and public assistance payments increased from $1.0 billion to $3.2 billion.

After the uninterrupted nine-year decline, the number of poor rose in 1970 to 25.5 million, reflecting the economic

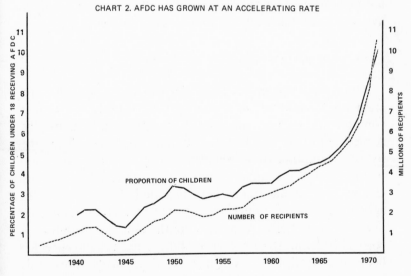

CHART 2. AFDC HAS GROWN AT AN ACCELERATING RATE

Source: U.S. Department of Health, Education, and Welfare

recession and consequent rising unemployment; AFDC rolls also continued to grow to 10.3 million at the end of 1971. Explanations of the rise differ, but there is agreement that female-headed families—who are the heart of the "welfare problem"—did not share fully in the unprecedented economic expansion of the 1960s. Poverty became increasingly concentrated in such families. In 1969 dependents of these families comprised only 12 percent of all children but 45 percent of those in poverty. A child in a female-headed family was three times as likely as a child in a male-headed family to be in poverty in 1960, but six times as likely in 1969 (54 percent in contrast to 9 percent).

Although one welfare family in six includes a father, two-thirds of these men are incapacitated; only about 5 percent of AFDC families include an able-bodied father. More than seven families in ten include only the mother. One family in ten includes neither the father nor mother, and the children live with a caretaker relative or in a foster home.

CAUSES OF AFDC'S GROWTH

Although originally expected to be a "transitional" program which would wither away as the contributory insurance components were broadened, AFDC increased dramatically. A plethora of reasons have accounted for the rise. The futility of attempting to ascribe cardinal or even ordinal importance to the causes in so complex an area should be obvious. Important national trends have included the decline of the agricultural sector, which contributed greatly to population mobility, especially from the south, and urbanization. A corollary of industrialization, mobility, and urbanization has been the decline of extended families, which previously looked after their own. A number of other, more specific, contributing forces can, however, be identified. Population has grown and family patterns have changed; eligibility has been broadened; welfare agencies look more favorably on welfare recipients; public assistance has become more attractive relative to earnings; and the contributory elements have not taken over nearly as fast as AFDC has grown.

More Potential Recipients

Population growth could be expected to expand the welfare rolls over time, other things being equal. Between 1940 and 1970, total population increased over 50 percent, and the population fourteen years and under grew more than 80 percent. There have also been important alterations in family structure. Divorces, desertion, and illegitimacy have risen sharply since the mid-1930s. All such changes that leave a mother as head of the household increase the number of potential AFDC clients. While the rate of marriage per 1,000 population has been virtually unchanged since 1935, the divorce rate has doubled. Moreover, the average number of children involved per divorce decree has been rising steadily. Illegitimacy has increased even faster. Between 1940 and 1968, the illegitimacy rate more than tripled, from 7 to 24 illegitimate births per 1,000 women aged fifteen to forty-four, and the proportion of all births which are illegitimate rose from 1 in 25 to 1 in 10. Data on desertions and separations without court decree—the "poor man's divorce"—are imprecise; but the proportion of presently married women whose husband is absent has increased from 4.1 in 1950 to 5.8 percent in 1970. Overall, one of every four women ever married was not living with her husband in 1970 (Table 2).

But cause and effect cannot readily be disentangled. One interpretation views the AFDC program as a response to economic and social forces resulting from the rise of the single-parent family. However, the program itself may alter the na-

9

Table 2. Ever-married women not living with husband, 1950, 1960, 1970

| | Percent | | |
	1950	1960	1970
Total	100.0	100.0	100.0
Not living with husband	21.3	23.5	25.1
Husband absent	3.4	4.5	4.6
Widowed	15.2	15.8	16.0
Divorced	2.7	3.2	4.5

SOURCE: U.S. Bureau of the Census.

ture of the population at risk, as families modify their behavior to qualify for benefits. For example, an able-bodied man who cannot earn enough to support his family may not qualify for welfare. To provide income for them he may desert and enable them to qualify for assistance. Similarly, the father of an unborn child may not marry the mother so that she may qualify for assistance. AFDC may, therefore, encourage the very phenomenon to which it is a response.

Knowledge of the availability of and eligibility requirements for AFDC have also increased over time. Groups such as the National Welfare Rights Organization have publicized AFDC and urged potential recipients to apply. Neighborhood legal service agencies, some of which are sponsored by the Office of Economic Opportunity, have also heightened awareness of the AFDC program. Routine inquiries for the Medicaid program may result in a finding that an applicant is also eligible for assistance payments.

Legislative Action and Court Decisions

Federal legislation extended coverage to groups not previously eligible. The original act provided aid to the wife and children of a man who was absent or incapacitated. In 1961 children and parents who were dependent because of the unemployment of an employable parent were included

(AFDC Unemployed Parent). In mid-1969 a foster care component was added, and most states have also adopted a provision that permits children to receive assistance after age eighteen if attending school. These extensions of coverage added some 800,000 persons to AFDC rolls by 1970.

The Supreme Court has struck down two typical state provisions that prevented many persons from receiving AFDC. In 1968 the court ruled unconstitutional the "man in the house" rule which held a man living in an AFDC home responsible for the children's support; the decision precluded cutting off aid because the mother cohabited with a man not obligated by law to support the children.[3] The following year, the Court invalidated the residency requirement for public assistance, in effect in more than forty states.[4]

Rising Income Limits

As the income limits for receiving assistance have been raised, more families have been able to qualify. To determine eligibility for AFDC, states specify "standards of need" for various family sizes. However, most states do not pay in full the designated standard. In July 1970 only fourteen states paid 100 percent of predetermined needs, and six paid less than 50 percent. In July 1969 the federal law required states to make a cost-of-living adjustment in the standards. As the standard is increased, more families are eligible for assistance. A number of states lagged in making these adjustments and a few have reduced standards and actual payments, contravening the apparent interest of Congress. Federal threats to cut off funds could be ignored, since only once in the history of the Social Security Act has federal aid been stopped.

Income disregards authorized by federal law have become increasingly important. Since 1962 states have disregarded work expenses in determining eligibility and computing payments. By 1968 twenty-eight states had adopted a provision which permitted monthly earnings of up to $50 per child or $150 for the children in any family to be disregarded in determining eligibility. Since mid-1969 states have been required to exempt in determining an AFDC family's grant all work-connected expenses and the first $30 of monthly earnings, plus one-third of all additional income. They are also required to exempt full earnings of a child who is a full-time student or a part-time student not working at a full-time job. Because the disregards, other than work expenses, now in effect apply only to families already receiving AFDC, they are not likely to add more persons to the rolls; however, they allow recipients who would otherwise have been disqualified to remain on the rolls.

Role of Administration

Local welfare officials have hardly been neutral in the rise of AFDC. Along with changes in federal regulations, local welfare administrators have tended to display greater leniency in qualifying applicants. The proportion of applications accepted—the percent of all applications received which are approved for money payments—declined from 66 percent in 1948 to 54 percent in 1953. The rate of acceptances changed little over the next decade, but then started to rise and reached 81 percent in 1970. But the balance of the applications were not necessarily denied since some applicants move away or fail to keep an appointment and the public welfare agency takes no formal action either to approve or deny their applications. In 1970 approvals constituted 81 percent of all applications received, but 88 percent of those acted upon.

The trend toward easier qualification was not limited to any region. In Atlanta, for example, the rate rose between 1960 and 1968 from 35 percent to 72 percent; in Chicago, from 47 percent to 74 percent; in Memphis, from 26 percent to 73 percent; in New Orleans, from 22 percent to 62 percent; in New York City, from 56 percent to 78 percent; and in Philadelphia, from 49 percent to 73 percent.[5]

Although acceptance rates have generally increased significantly, approval of an application for AFDC is not automatic. One-fifth of the recipients in a national survey in 1967 had at some time applied unsuccessfully for assistance; of these, one-third had been rejected at least twice. Whatever the greater ease to qualify, bureaucratic delays in processing persist as a deterrent to entering the relief system. The 1967 survey found that the time-lapse between application and receipt of first check was less than one month for two-fifths of the respondents, from one to two months for another two-fifths, and more than two months for the other one-fifth.[6]

The Department of Health, Education, and Welfare and the New York State Department of Social Services also examined the role of administration in increasing AFDC caseloads. In the eleven major cities studied, the extent of utilization of AFDC by the city's poor population was associated positively with the rate of caseworker turnover, the relative youth of caseworkers, and the caseworkers' "recipient orientation," and inversely with the caseworkers' "professionalism."[7] The evidence is persuasive that caseworkers can ration welfare. "Professional" caseworkers consider the needs of both the applicant and the agency and, therefore, are better rationers.

Staff turnover, age, orientation, and professionalism may be the chicken, however, and increases in the welfare rolls, the egg. An initial rise in the number of applications or recipients, for example, is likely to result in the hiring of new staff members or an overload on existing staff, either of which is likely, in turn, to further expand the rolls. New workers will

13

probably be younger and more lenient in assessing applications; an overburdened staff is an example of false economy to the extent that they approve applications too readily, simply to avoid building backlogs.

Increasing Attractiveness of AFDC

Finally, the broader attractiveness of AFDC relative to other sources of income was a basic condition for the growth of the program. Population growth and extensions of coverage were necessary to allow more people to qualify for assistance. But the sufficient condition has been the preference for AFDC. As the federal government assumed a larger share of the burden, states became less reluctant to qualify individuals for aid; as the level of aid also grew, participation in the program became increasingly preferable for those eligible. Between 1947 and 1962, average AFDC payments and spendable average weekly earnings of all private employees each rose by about two-thirds. But between 1963 and 1971, the average AFDC payment increased by 67 percent; the average spendable earnings of all private employees by only 42 percent (Chart 3). Significant increases in food stamps and medical care benefits for AFDC clients—not reflected in the cash payments—have tilted the balance even more in the favor of welfare.

Even for those who want to be self-supporting, a considerable work effort is required to equal available public assistance. In most big cities more than two full weeks' work would be necessary to match monthly cash payments alone for a young mother with one child (Table 3). When the food stamps, health care, and perhaps public housing benefits are added, the necessary income from earnings to equal real public assistance income must also increase, as it does again when child care and other work-related expenses are consid-

CHART 3. AFDC PAYMENTS HAVE INCREASED FASTER THAN EARNINGS*

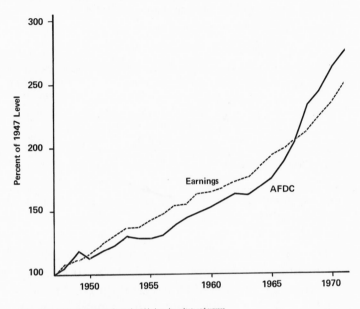

*Spendable average weekly earnings for worker with three dependents and average
monthly payment per AFDC recipient.

Source: U.S. Departments of Health, Education, and Welfare, and Labor

ered. And for older women the additional responsibilities and
costs of larger families are unlikely to be balanced by a pro-
portionate rise in earnings capacity.

Welfare can be, therefore, an attractive option to self-
support and, once in "the system," a mother with small
children may have little incentive to attempt to earn her way
out. Even if her income rises enough so that she no longer
qualifies for cash payments, she may still receive the add-ons.
Only at relatively high income levels do all benefits cease.

A study by the General Accounting Office (GAO) found
that a typical AFDC mother with three children can earn up
to $579 monthly in Los Angeles and $207 monthly in Den-

15

Table 3. Comparison of 1970 welfare payments and average wages for 16- to 19-year-old females in slum areas, 1969

	Maximum monthly state AFDC payments, mother with one child	Median hourly wage	Hours of work to earn equivalent monthly AFDC payment
Atlanta	$ 71	$1.53	46
Chicago	228	1.68	136
Detroit	181	1.68	108
Houston	113	1.38	82
New York City	219	2.00	110
Los Angeles	148	1.75	85

SOURCE: U.S. Bureau of Labor Statistics, and U.S. Department of Health, Education, and Welfare.

ver before any reduction is made in her benefit and up to $1,074 monthly in Los Angeles and up to $750 monthly in Denver before termination of all payment. In Los Angeles she may still qualify for medical and dental benefits after other assistance is stopped.

In order to ascertain the effect of earning on assistance payments, the GAO followed up some welfare mothers in Los Angeles who had obtained jobs. For the average family, the value of earnings and assistance totaled $735 monthly— her earnings of $433 plus welfare benefits of $302 ($221 in cash, $24 in a food stamp bonus, and $57 worth of free medical and dental care). When her actual work expenses of $266 ($54 for payroll deductions, $25 for food and incidentals, $80 for transportation, and $107 for child care) were subtracted, her net monthly gain from working was $167, and her net monthly cash and in-kind income was $469.[8]

The relative attractiveness of AFDC is not based solely on finances. The stigma of welfare has certainly deterred many eligible persons from applying for assistance. However, it is likely that such reluctance has diminished. On a national basis, an increasingly large proportion of the population receives nonwelfare government income support. Cash paid in the form of retirement, disability, and survivor benefits; unemployment benefits; veterans benefits; temporary disability benefits; workmen's compensation; and public assistance rocketed from $3.6 billion in 1945 to $25.9 billion in 1960 to $64.3 billion in 1970. The number of beneficiaries rose from 9 million in 1945 to 30 million in 1960 to 50 million—nearly one-quarter of the population—in 1970. When government handouts are allocated to giant corporations in financial straits and to millionaire farmers, a poor mother with children is not likely to feel less worthy of aid nor more reticent in seeking it. One conscious attempt to decrease the difficulty of applying for, and stigma of receiving, assistance has been frustrated. Since 1969 states have been allowed to use a "simplified" method of determining eligibility, relying solely on applicants' statements and not verifying information independently. Although such a system was supposed to be in effect in twenty-two states in early 1971, the GAO found that local directors had modified the simplified system, so that there was little difference between it and the traditional method of determining eligibility.[9]

As the proportion of residents who are AFDC recipients has increased, nationally, and especially in a number of states and central cities, the acceptability of relief has also grown. California and New York contained 14 percent of all AFDC families in 1948 and 30 percent in 1970, although they contain under one-fifth of the entire population. About half of all welfare recipients reside in central cities of 100,000 or more, where they comprise an increasingly substantial proportion of the total population. In February 1971 the AFDC

17

rolls included more than one-tenth of the population of New York, Philadelphia, Baltimore, Boston, St. Louis, and New Orleans.[10]

Countervailing Forces

The replacement of public assistance by contributory elements of the Social Security Act has proceeded slowly. A decline in mortality at birth and increasing longevity have reduced the number of orphans. Although the proportion of all orphans receiving benefits or payments rose between 1940 and 1966 from about 12 percent to about 81 percent, AFDC's share declined as OASDHI and veterans programs assumed most of the burden. In 1966 AFDC assisted only 5 percent, OASDHI 53 percent, and veterans programs 23 percent of all orphans. It has been estimated that in the absence of other income support programs, more than 600,000 paternal orphans might have received AFDC in 1966 instead of only one-quarter of that number.[11]

In 1969 about 8 percent of the AFDC families also received social security. Similarly, the broadening of participation in OASDHI also reduced the number of dependents of incapacitated workers who receive AFDC. The "blanketing in" of the children of dead and disabled men under social security and the rise in illegitimacy, desertion, and divorce have led to a dramatic shift in the distribution of AFDC families according to the father's status. In 1942 the father in three of every five AFDC families was dead or incapacitated; nearly all the rest were not married to the mother, separated, or divorced. By 1971, however, fewer than one in five was dead, incapacitated, or unemployed; nearly three-quarters were not married to the mother, separated, or divorced.

Recurrent allegations that welfare rolls could be pared by weeding out "cheaters" have not been supported by facts.

18

The most recent national investigation of AFDC eligibility, in April 1971, revealed that 5.6 percent of the families should not have been receiving benefits and that 15 percent of the eligible families received overpayment and 10 percent underpayment. The errors that led to ineligibility or incorrect payment were due equally to agency and client mistakes. However, cases involving fraud were reported to be very few. These findings are similar to those of a national study made in 1963.

There was a steady rise in AFDC clientele during its first three and a half decades and this growth has accelerated during the past decade. Population growth, changes in family structure, broadened eligibility, eased financial requirements, and less stringent administration contributed to the dramatic increases of AFDC. But in the final analysis, the decision to seek assistance was primarily stimulated by the increasing attractiveness of AFDC relative to other sources of income.

NOTES

1. U.S. Congress, Senate Committee on Finance, *Hearings on H.R. 1, Social Security Amendments of 1971*, 92nd Cong., 1st Sess. (Washington: Government Printing Office, 1971), pp. 52–55.

2. Blanche O. Coll, *Perspectives in Public Welfare: A History* (Washington: Government Printing Office, 1969), and Bruno Stein, *On Relief: The Economics of Poverty and Public Welfare* (New York: Basic Books, 1971), chapter 2.

3. *King* v. *Smith*, 392 U.S. 309.

4. *Shapiro* v. *Thompson*, 394 U.S. 618.

5. U.S. Congress, House Committee on Ways and Means. *Report of Findings of Special Review of Aid to Families with Dependent Children in New York City*, 91st Cong., 1st Sess. (Washington: Government Printing Office, 1969), p. A–23.

6. U.S. Department of Health, Education, and Welfare, Social and Rehabilitation Service, National Center for Social Statistics, *1967 AFDC Study, Preliminary Report of Findings From Mail Questionnaire*, January 1969, p. 12.

7. U.S. Congress, House Committee on Ways and Means, *Report of Findings of Special Review of Aid to Families with Dependent Children in New York City*, 91st Cong., 1st Sess. (Washington: Government Printing Office, 1969), pp. 55–56.

8. Comptroller General of the United States, *Problems in Accomplishing Objectives of the Work Incentive Program (WIN)*, September 1971, pp. 29–31.

9. Comptroller General of the United States, *Comparison of the Simplified and Traditional Methods of Determining Eligibility For Aid To Families With Dependent Children*, July 1971.

10. Harold Coleman, "Public Assistance in Large Cities, February 1971," NCSS Brief Report 71–2, in *Public Assistance Statistics, February 1971*, U.S. Department of Health, Education, and Welfare, 1971, pp. 1–5.

11. David Eppley, "Decline in the Number of AFDC Orphans: 1935–1966," *Welfare in Review* (September–October 1968): 7.

2

Welfare and In-Kind Benefits

WHY IN-KIND PROGRAMS?

The poor need money. But like the rest of the population, they need much more than that. Among the many new responsibilities that the government has assumed since New Deal days are programs that benefit the poor. To help farmers unload their surplus production, some commodities have been turned over to the poor. Government entry into the housing business has included the building of dwellings for the poor. The in-kind programs in aid of the poor are, however, more than spin-offs or by-products of general social programs. Diverse rationalizations have been advanced to justify assistance over and above cash offered to the poor. The three major arguments are (1) that special services offered to the poor may change their behavior and motivate them to become independent; (2) that in-kind goods or services have to be delivered *directly* to the poor because the open market operates unresponsively in serving them; and (3) that the earmarking of funds for special purposes focuses attention on the specific needs of the poor and is an effective strategy for expanding the level of resources allocated to them. While these arguments apply to the poor as a group, they are especially relevant to welfare recipients and those dependent on means-tested public aid.

To Change Behavior

To argue that those who are economically dependent need to change their behavior as well as their economic circumstances is to assume that they have special problems. American society seems to be most preoccupied with those personal problems that are presumed to inhibit an individual's capacity to participate in the labor force. When special circumstances arise that are beyond the individual's control (such as blindness, disability, or old age), a compassionate and humane society is prepared to offer aid. By this standard not all the poor are considered "deserving." Any assistance offered to those whose discretionary actions are believed to contribute to their dire circumstances and dependency—for example, desertion and illegitimacy—has traditionally been given grudgingly. One can note a trend toward expanding the entitlements of the "undeserving" poor, but pressure has also been exerted to alter the behavior of these recipients to assure that they do not receive public aid longer than is necessary. This requires special programs that can contribute to their economic independence.

To Improve the Allocation of Resources

It is not always economically efficient to give those on welfare money to secure the goods they require. The argument seems compelling and simple. Medical care facilities and shelter provisions are in short supply. Increasingly, the resources available to welfare recipients are unlikely, in the short run, to produce a greater supply of housing or medical care. Instead, the pressure for these services inflates market prices for them, thus making it more difficult for those on welfare to secure access to them. Services that society judges crucial to the well-being of families can be distributed more efficiently in the form of in-kind programs.

Certain goods or services are essential, and hence public policy is concerned with their equitable distribution. They should not be controlled exclusively by free market operation on the basis of wealth but rather on that of need. Thus, an egalitarian argument supports the efficiency rationale.

To Provide More Aid

The final rationale is based on an assessment of political realities. It is assumed that to improve the economic well-being of welfare recipients, earmarked and in-kind programs have more political appeal than general cash grants, on the pragmatic grounds that they build political support for specific programs. The construction industry benefits from the growth of public housing; the farmer benefits from the food stamp program; the medical profession gains from government financing of health care; and, finally, feeding the hungry appeals to basic human instincts. These groups have a special stake in an assured market during periods when housing construction is low and when surpluses are produced which can threaten the price structure of the food market. The political axiom deduced from these examples is simply that the program is likely to grow and receive support if influential groups have a stake in it or it appeals to groups with influence. In addition, in-kind benefits can create consumer coalitions. This can occur when benefits are allocated to a wider spectrum of the population, including groups that are not on welfare. A broadening of the base, however, frequently leaves out the most needy or results in a skimping of services to the poor. It is also easier to secure support for special circumstances that capture the political imagination by their appeal to citizen compassion or to broadly accepted norms. A program to prevent hunger, or to assure that children have an adequate diet, or to provide shelter to residents of dilapidated housing, or to deliver health care to the sick, or to train people so that they may become economically independent can draw together a political coalition of interests that would not cooperate on the more abstract issue of "helping the poor." In short, then, a pluralistic approach, in which a variety of programs is inspired by a variety of motives, may lead to more total help for those on welfare as well as for the near poor. Moreover, a combination of in-kind programs may appear to create less work disincentive than an equivalent amount of cash.

These broad aims find expression in specific programs for those in receipt of cash grants. The social services, including manpower training programs, seem directed primarily at changing the poor and protecting society. The in-kind programs of food, medical care, and shelter seem to have been initiated partly from a conviction that those on welfare could secure more basic requirements if these were provided in the form of in-kind benefits added on top of cash payments. The argument for greater efficiency in reaching those in need of medical care and housing requires no further elaboration. It seems clear that a marginal increase in cash payments for welfare recipients would not enable them to alter the market supply of housing and medical care facilities and services. If one wants them to be better housed and to receive better medical care, then it is necessary to provide these services more directly. These assumptions have clearly been accepted since World War II in the case of public housing and even earlier in the case of "free" city clinics for the provision of medical care.

The distinction between cash payments and in-kind aid is becoming blurred as individuals have been acquiring greater freedom in utilizing in-kind assistance. Those seeking medical care, for example, are increasingly free to choose their own doctor, though payments are made directly to the doctor (the vendor of the service). But the degree of freedom is limited. The Medicaid patient is not free to make use of the medical outlays for any other purpose. Unless he uses the funds for health care, he loses any claims on the welfare resources. Therefore the distinction between cash payments and in-kind aid remains crucial.

Finally, commodity programs cannot be justified solely on the grounds of efficiency. Since they create a new administrative mechanism for the distribution of food, they create additional costs. The food stamp program relies upon the established institutional arrangements for distributing food, but here, too, administrative complexity is added through the need to arrange for the purchase of and reimbursement for stamps. Advocates of the program justify food stamps on the grounds that more resources can be earmarked for those in need. Also, they argue, a general cash grant may not assure that the family spends the funds specifically for food.

The motives behind the creation of an in-kind program are multiple and complex. But whatever the validity of these arguments, and whatever the priorities different groups assign to each, the in-kind, means-tested benefits in aid of the poor and near-poor have grown rapidly in recent years and now carry a price tag virtually equal to assistance paid in cash. In fiscal 1971, when outlays for cash assistance were $9.8 billion, in-kind costs amounted to $9.6 billion (Chart 4). Federal outlays for in-kind benefits are actually greater than for money payments.

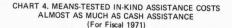

CHART 4. MEANS-TESTED IN-KIND ASSISTANCE COSTS
ALMOST AS MUCH AS CASH ASSISTANCE
(For Fiscal 1971)

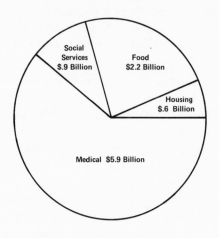

Total = $9.6 Billion

Source: U.S. Office of Management and Budget

THE SOCIAL SERVICES

The 1962 Amendments to the Social Security Act heralded a new development in welfare policy for the United States. President Kennedy, in supporting this legislation, promised that the new approach would bring "rehabilitation instead of relief." Social services were to be the primary vehicle to implement this rehabilitation strategy.

Social services include such diverse activities that they defy definition. Their scope can be indicated in terms of a catalog of illustrative activities, suggesting the range of programs, or in terms of broad social objectives. The items included in any laundry list are arbitrary, since the criteria for inclusion are uncertain; yet some general consensus emerges. At one ex-

26

treme are such inclusive activities as counseling and at the other specific activities such as homemaker and day care services. These activities are sometimes characterized, respectively, as "soft" and "hard" programs. Broad social objectives may include "self-support" or "strengthening family life," and all the activities performed by a social worker to promote these objectives are defined as social services. Thus the process of determining whether someone has a problem, even if nothing can be or is done to relieve it, is regarded as a social service. By this definition HEW claimed that 84 percent of all AFDC families received services during 1970.[1] These included a wide variety of activities (Chart 5).

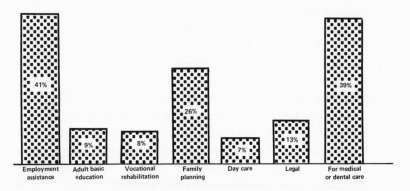

CHART 5. AFDC FAMILIES RECEIVE A WIDE VARIETY OF SERVICES
(For 1970)

Source: U.S. Department of Health, Education, and Welfare

The process of sorting out an individual's problems, offering some counsel and advice, and referring him to other appropriate community services is the essence of social services as interpreted by the 1962 Social Security Amendments. The five-year experiment that was initiated with the 1962 amendments was essentially an effort to apply the experiences of professional social workers in voluntary agencies to a mass public program, and it was presumably based on a series of demonstration projects authorized by the 1956 Social Security Amendments. Reports from these earliest loosely evaluated demonstrations offered some encouraging evidence that the approach was feasible and effective.[2] No systematic evaluation of the social services undertaken under the 1962 amendments is available, but it is nevertheless possible to review some of the problems encountered.

By 1967, when the initial authorization of the 1962 amendments was due to expire, very little progress had been made in clarifying the needed components of the prescribed social services, let alone the effects they had in encouraging employability among AFDC families. Selected studies were discouraging. For example, the Community Service Society, a voluntary social work agency, in collaboration with the New York City Department of Social Services attempted to determine the effectiveness of case work intervention in preventing individual and family disorganization and in assisting families to achieve economic independence and adequate "social functioning." A randomly selected experimental group, all newly dependent on public assistance, and a control group were studied during a fourteen-month period. The experimental families received a wide range of services, while the control group received only routine public assistance visits. Structured interviews provided the basis for the evaluation, which concluded that the functioning and conditions of these two groups remained essentially similar.[3] Considering how uncertain were the undefined aims of "social functioning," the vagueness of the conclusion should not be surprising.

More useful for the consideration of employability among welfare recipients are studies concerned with the relationship between services and employment. For example, four general conclusions can be drawn from a 1969 review of welfare in New York City:

1. New York City relies upon special programs and projects in rendering its social services, but relatively few welfare recipients participate in the programs. In more than six years of experience, only 46,320 had enrolled in these innovative programs, and even this modest number included duplications of recipients who enrolled in two or more programs. By contrast, in 1969 alone there were approximately 140,000 families in receipt of AFDC benefits.

2. The available evidence makes it abundantly clear that priority is not given to AFDC recipients, even in agencies with which the Department of Social Services has ongoing cooperative relationships. Of the children enrolled in day care centers, which are financed 90 percent by the Department of Social Services, only one-sixth were current public assistance recipients and one-third were former welfare clients.

3. A prime function of social services is presumably to assess the problems confronting the family and to determine the employability status of clients. But only 16 percent of all adults enrolled in New York City's welfare program received an employability evaluation, and only 8 percent of all AFDC adults were so classified. Though a very elaborate procedure had been created for sorting and categorizing, only a modest proportion of the total AFDC population was included. By these measures, New York City has failed to carry out the intent of the 1967 amendments, establishing the Work Incentive (WIN) program.

4. Finally, there is much looseness in the administration of "social services" because of the attrition between contact, referral, and receipt of service. Only about 10 percent of the AFDC cases were referred to the state employment service. Of 43 persons referred to the state employment service, 33 were seen by an employment counselor and 22 were referred

29

to training and jobs. A follow-up of these 22 cases showed that one was terminated because of employment and three others were already employed full-time and presumably may already have been at the time of referral.[4]

A home interview survey conducted for the HEW report by the National Opinion Research Center of 616 randomly selected AFDC women in New York City buttresses the pattern of attrition indicated by this review. About 45 percent of the clients interviewed reported that they had discussed employment with their case worker or other personnel in the welfare department. Of these, 5 percent reported that they had been referred to an employer and 7 percent reported referral to a training program; an additional 9 percent said that they had at some time been in a job training or basic education program, but "only 2 percent said the training helped them to get a job."[5]

In short, there is widespread slippage between contact, referral, and the actual receipt of services. Other agencies that formally cooperate with the State Department of Social Services assign low priority to welfare clients. National evidence confirms the New York City experience.

Not only do social services fail to reach most AFDC recipients but the effectiveness of these services has also been questioned. A review of thirteen studies devoted to the evaluation of social work intervention suggested that the mode of intervention which was sought as a model was not only of doubtful effectiveness for welfare clients but was equally in doubt when applied to other populations.[6]

Concluding that case work was not an effective method for intervening in the problems of welfare families and other low-income families, the Community Service Society in 1971 abandoned case-work practice in Harlem. The announcement that a well-established and highly reputed case-work institution had forsaken case work in the ghetto because of its ineffectiveness in aiding the poor no doubt disturbed the social work profession. But Congress had already several years earlier lost confidence in these services and the contribution they might make toward the economic independence of welfare clients.

An administrative review of the experience since the 1962 amendments suggested further difficulties. Most of the services for the public assistance program seemed to be devoted to the determination of eligibility. Efforts to conduct a social study of the AFDC population in order to classify recipients according to the services they needed resulted in confusion rather than aid to the clients, and the total impact of the study was negative. The inordinate amount of paper work generated by the exercise contributed to delays in the handling of applications and made more difficult the task of responding to emergency requests for aid. Thus, the efforts to learn about the problems of families proved self-defeating in a large bureaucratic setting and in the end hampered rather than facilitated the delivery of services. The process produced very few referrals to other community agencies, and the caseworkers were neither rendering the services themselves nor helping their clients to receive them from other community resources. An approach to social services which had been developed by voluntary social welfare agencies working with a limited clientele could not be converted into a large-scale national program manned by inexperienced staff.

An overhaul of the delivery system was clearly mandatory if services were to play a role in encouraging employment among welfare clients. And, indeed, change was in the air, not so much because of the failures of the 1962 amendments but because developments in the war on poverty made them redundant. The Office of Economic Opportunity's community action programs emphasized concrete and specific services such as legal programs, day care, Head Start, other forms of compensatory education, and manpower training. The 1967 Social Security Amendments reflected this change in emphasis. Services were to be more concrete and specifically related to the problems of family structure and work behavior.

The failure of the 1962 amendments not only suggested the need for more concrete and work-related services but also implied that if the thrust of those amendments had been misplaced, then the whole organization and structure of services needed to be redirected as well. At the heart of the 1962 amendments was the assumption that a thorough investigation of the family circumstances was necessary in determining whether a client was eligible for welfare, and that the information secured in this way could be used as a basis for diagnosing a client's problems and for later counseling and referral where necessary. Yet, however logically compelling the argument might have been for combining the eligibility review with an assessment of the client's problems, the effort proved abortive.

Once it had been demonstrated that eligibility was not crucial for the rendering of service, then it seemed to follow that the process of determining eligibility could be simplified and undertaken by clerical workers as a routine task and that cash payments could be separated from services. If cash and services could be split, then it also seemed to follow that there was no compelling reason to limit services only to those individuals who received public assistance. Indeed the 1962 amendments proposed not only that services be available to those on welfare but also that they be used as a strategy for preventing dependency. Thus the program could be generalized to other groups in addition to the welfare population. In brief, then, the experience with the 1962 and 1967 amendments suggested that eligibility determination should be simplified, cash be separated from service, and services be made more generally available to a wider population.[7]

More than half the states have made substantial progress in separating eligibility determination from provision of social services. But the burden of keeping up with the flood of applications has hindered further progress, despite prompting by HEW. Separation is generally supported by the states, according to HEW, but it has been effected too recently and incompletely for an adequate assessment. Matching formulae are important in determining the allocation of personnel to determine eligibility and render services after separation. Because the federal government foots 75 percent of the services bill, but only 50 percent for eligibility, the former may be relatively overstaffed and the latter understaffed. Moreover, administrative experience suggests how difficult it is, in practice, to implement the separation of cash and services, although the guidelines suggest that 75 percent matching funds would be available only when such separation took place. While there is not much experience with either the declaration or the separation of cash and services, it has been increasingly clear that the services favored by the 1967 amendments to the Social Security Act presented new difficulties, including the high cost of day care programs. More than abstract conceptual problems are involved. For example, should day care serve as a compensatory education program, as in the case of Head Start, or as a custodial child care program designed simply to enable mothers to work? How this "choice" is decided greatly affects the cost of the program. The separate objectives of enhancing the future earnings of the child and the present earnings of the parent are awkwardly in conflict. Manpower training programs have also encountered difficulties because they are responsive to the circumstances of the clients rather than to local labor market conditions.

A review of the past decade reveals the continuing frustration of the House Ways and Means Committee in seeking an effective service strategy. Disappointed in the effects of the 1962 provisions, the Committee concluded five years later that its approach to social services had proved a failure, and it recognized instead the need to prepare AFDC clients for work. But in 1970 it affirmed, and in 1971 reaffirmed, its disappointment with the results of work experience efforts. Day care costs seemed high, manpower training programs seemed ineffective, and legal services designed to protect the poor from inappropriate work requirements or infringement of their "rights" to benefits proved to be politically controversial.

In summary, then, the past decade has been one of experimentation with different attempts to define and clarify the nature and scope of social services. The trend has been toward rendering services that are generally work-related. Day care, family planning, and manpower training programs are the major examples of the new directions that are advocated. But the new strategies are either costly or unproved as encouraging economic independence for welfare recipients. Other conceptions of social services have emerged as well; legal services, for example, were designed not to change the poor but to protect them and to assure that they received the benefits to which they were entitled.

That the newer approaches to social service will prove more effective than the old case-work method in "rehabilitating" the poor and inducing them to become economically independent remains a matter of faith. The limited experience with the new work-related efforts does not justify optimism about their promise as an effective strategy. Experimentation will no doubt continue, but each promising road has, in the end, proved frustrating to the advocates of "rehabilitation instead of relief."

IN-KIND PROGRAMS FOR NECESSITIES

Receipt of welfare provides an automatic passport (in most cases) to free or subsidized food, medical care, and shelter. Although these services are directed to those on welfare, they are not limited to this group. A review of the legislative development of the in-kind programs clearly suggests that extension beyond the group on welfare was intentional. Whether eligible welfare recipients make use of these service is a neglected empirical question.

Food

✗ Programs to feed the needy in the United States can be traced to Section 32 of the 1937 amendments to the Agricultural Adjustment Act. The national school lunch program, initiated in 1947, provides grants to states for "the establishment, maintenance, operation and expansion of non-profit school-lunch programs." Schools are required to serve lunches free or at reduced prices to needy students who are unable to pay the full cost. A food stamp program in effect prior to World War II was renewed by a series of pilot projects under an executive order by President Kennedy in 1961.

From these modest beginnings the programs have been expanded during the past decade and accelerated during the 1970s. Since 1967 the food stamp program has attracted much political interest; federal financing rose fifteenfold, to $1.6 billion, between 1966 and 1971. By 1971 mean-tested in-kind food assistance totaled $2.2 billion, an amount equal to more than one-fifth of aggregate cash payments during the same year (Table 4). Nearly all the benefits from means-tested programs accrued to the poor in 1971, as did more than one-quarter of the over $700 million spent on programs with no means test. Continued growth was anticipated, with federal expenditures expected to rise another $1 billion to $3.2 billion by 1973, reaching over thirteen million persons.

Table 4. Most food assistance is means-tested and goes to the poor

	Outlays (millions)		Proportion of outlays for poor, 1971 (%)
	1969	1971	
Means-tested, total	$579	$2,216	92
Free and reduced price breakfasts and lunches	46	325	92
Food stamps	250	1,577	92
Commodity distribution to families	282	314	93
Not means-tested, total	621	729	28

SOURCE: U.S. Department of Agriculture.

Much of the controversy in 1971 about overhauling the welfare system focused on food programs. Trying to integrate these programs with its welfare reform proposals, the administration proposed cuts for some recipients and more liberal provisions for others, but Congress endorsed only the latter. The result was an expanded food program, though some restrictions emerged, disqualifying perhaps one million persons from receiving food stamps. First, to preclude "hippies" and students from receiving benefits, unrelated individuals living in a household were held to disqualify the entire household. Second, able-bodied adult recipients were required to register for and accept employment—at the applicable minimum wage or $1.30 per hour—as a condition of receiving food stamps.

The expansions were even more significant. Whereas widely varying state standards for public assistance had typically been used to determine eligibility for food stamps, the poverty level (in 1970, almost $4,000 for a family of four) was established nationwide as the lowest ceiling for eligibility. This substantially raised the standards, since welfare levels exceed the poverty line in only a few states. And since eligibility for cash assistance automatically qualified a family for food programs, the subsidies offered were also liberalized. Food stamps were to be free to a family of four with a monthly income of less than $30. For others, the benefit was to be sufficient to allow purchase of the Department of Agriculture's "nutritionally adequate" diet at a cost no more than 30 percent of the family's income. New eligibility standards were estimated to qualify 1.7 million more persons for benefits. Refocusing the food programs more directly toward families, setting the poverty level as the minimum income ceiling, and establishing a work requirement were all important steps in integrating the food programs with cash assistance programs, in line with welfare reform.

Child nutrition programs, which include both means-tested and nonmeans-tested components, have developed along similar lines, with Congress rebuffing administration attempts to prune back the program. The nonmeans-tested aspects have grown very little during the past few years, while the means-tested segment grew from about $40 million in 1969 to over $300 million in 1971 and was expected to reach $580 million in 1973. Under the former, the federal government donates commodities to schools and subsidizes the milk and school lunches purchased by all children. Poor children were estimated to receive more than one-fifth of these benefits. Under the latter, an additional federal outlay covers most or all of the rest of the cost of school breakfasts and lunches for children who demonstrate need. Over 90 percent of these expenditures were estimated to benefit poor children.

In the fall of 1971 the administration attempted to restrict federal expenditures under the program by cutting the average federal reimbursement rate per meal and by restricting eligibility for free and reduced-price lunches to children from families with an annual income below the poverty level. Congress rejected these "savings" and in a joint resolution increased the federal reimbursement rate per meal; permitted the continued use of local welfare eligibility standards, as of October 1970, for all free and reduced-price lunches; and allowed states to continue to use Department of Agriculture funds for school breakfast programs, as well as school lunch programs.

Still pending before Congress is legislation to provide free daily meals to all children regardless of their means. While the adoption of a universal school lunch program may be unlikely soon, legislative sentiment has favored liberalization of the program in the past and is clearly opposed to any restriction of the current effort, either in terms of funds expended or target population subsidized.

Health Care

During the 1950s, experiments were tried with medical vendor payments for welfare recipients. The federal government encouraged the development of such vendor payments, first by originating the principle, then by establishing separate matching for medical care payments, and finally by setting a general averaging formula whereby cash and vendor payments for medical care could be integrated.

The scope of medical care was expanded during the succeeding decade, at least in principle, by providing that medical care should be available to all the needy and not only to recipients of federal categorical aid. The Kerr–Mills program had established in 1954 the goal of reaching all the needy aged. But the effort was frustrated by the states that simply transferred all their old-age assistance recipients to the new category called "Medical Assistance for the Aged." In 1965 Congress extended medical care benefits to needy persons excluded from public assistance because they did not meet certain eligibility requirements. The intent of Congress was to extend comprehensive medical services by 1972 to all the medically indigent. A variety of factors has frustrated the achievement of this goal: abuse by medical vendors, administrative inability to curb medical costs, and the broadening of eligibility to families and individuals with low and moderate earnings. The result has been that medical costs and expenditures have increased enormously. Total federal-state medical vendor payments in fiscal 1971 amounted to $6.3 billion, a more than fourfold rise in six years. In 1965 medical vendor payments equaled 38 percent of cash welfare budgets, rising to 62 percent in 1971. To arrest the swelling Medicaid outlays, Congress limited eligibility to families whose incomes were no more than 133 percent of AFDC payments; and the states could further limit the coverage of medical care provided to the medically needy. Present policy is designed to restrict Medicaid to public assistance recipients, except for children and the elderly.

By sharply restricting eligibility and coverage, Medicaid was unable, even though it reached those above the welfare line, to build an effective political constituency. Therefore, it followed the usual pattern of welfare programs, whereby unpopular efforts tend to reach a plateau and then to erode in the quality of benefits, the number of beneficiaries, or both. In the case of Medicaid, the cutbacks were severe and were precipitated by rapidly rising costs of medical care and the difficulty experienced in expanding medical facilities. A review of the history of the program concludes that Medicaid "is destined to be phased out during the next decade."[8]

Medicaid's uneasy role as a health care program and as an extended aspect of income maintenance will need to be resolved before a future direction can be sorted out.

Shelter

Federal housing assistance for low-income families has expanded dramatically over the last decade. By mid-1971 there were 1.8 million housing units built, rented, or purchased with government subsidies for occupancy by low-income families. According to the best available estimates total federal annual housing subsidies in 1971 exceeded $1 billion.[9]

Public housing, the most important program, accounted for more than half of the subsidized units available in 1971. Dating back to the Housing Act of 1937, this program provides annual contributions from the federal government to amortize the development costs of publicly owned and operated housing and to pay extra subsidies for selected groups of tenants who cannot pay even the reduced rentals charged in this housing. Eligibility for public housing is limited to low-income families by locally established rules. The median annual family income of residents in 1969 was only $1,714 for those with an elderly head and $3,712 for others. Ninety-five percent of the former group and more than 40 percent of the latter were receiving public assistance benefits. The average annual subsidy per unit of public housing is between $500 and $800, depending on the age and type of unit.

A conceptually promising effort was initiated in 1965 with the rent supplement program. Instead of limiting assistance to public housing, the rent supplement program shifted the responsibility for building and operating low-rent housing projects from the local housing authorities to private groups.

Congress restricted rent supplements to families that would qualify for public housing.

The rent supplement program provides direct contributions making up the difference between the rents charged in specially designated units and one-fourth of the tenants' incomes. There were over 60,000 rent-supplemented units in 1971, most of them built under other subsidy programs and using the rent supplement to reach the lower-income families. More than nine of every ten families receiving rent supplements earned $4,000 or less annually, according to a 1969 survey. More than three-fifths were public assistance recipients. Subsidies under the rent supplement program amounted to about $900 per unit annually, an even larger overall subsidy than provided by housing.

Forty percent of public housing clients and 20 percent of rent supplement recipients are drawn from the welfare rolls. Altogether, perhaps as many as half a million households on public assistance also received housing subsidies in 1969. The newer programs tend to help the working poor more than they do welfare recipients.

ELIGIBILITY CRITERIA

In-kind programs for basic necessities are not exclusively oriented to those on welfare. Indeed, many of the programs were explicitly designed to reach beyond the welfare level and each program established a somewhat different income cut-off point. Although Gunnar Myrdal observed nearly a decade ago that "American economic and social policies show a perverse tendency to favor groups that are above the level of the most needy,"[10] the rising costs of these programs have created pressures to reduce both the coverage and the scope of services.

The programs under consideration are no exception in offering assistance to those above the welfare benefit levels. And these programs share the persistent conflict over where to fix eligibility levels. Eligibility for housing subsidies was initially set substantially above the welfare line, and the new housing programs during the 1960s were geared to help the near-poor or those with modest incomes rather than the poor themselves. Indeed, those with no income or a very low income cannot qualify for housing programs. Medicaid reached deeply into lower-middle-income groups, but inflation in medical care costs pressed Congress to place a lid on eligibility. Thus far, no congressional pressure has been created to establish any income ceiling in public housing similar to that developed in Medicaid. Of the major in-kind measures, only the food programs (except school lunches) have been oriented solely to those at or below the welfare level. But in recent years, national standards for food stamps have also been pegged above the welfare line.

Qualifying for cash assistance is normally a passport to automatic eligibility for means-tested in-kind programs, but possession does not necessarily mean that the holders of the passport exploit their right to travel. A major lesson of the antipoverty program is that the poor frequently do not participate in programs on their behalf, and the available information, though fragmented, suggests wide geographic variation in relief recipients' participation in means-tested programs.

Some eighteen million persons received Medicaid benefits in fiscal 1971, nearly 80 percent of whom also received public assistance, while slightly over 20 percent did not. Of the former fourteen million, over one-third were aged, blind, or disabled; one-quarter were adults in families with dependent children; and two-fifths were dependent children. Of the four million nonwelfare recipients, the overwhelming majority were aged, disabled, blind, or children. Overall, the program was clearly directed to the aged, blind, disabled, and children (Chart 6.)

Persons who receive public assistance are automatically eligible for participation in the food stamp program, and

CHART 6. AFDC RECIPIENTS ACCOUNT FOR ONLY ONE-THIRD OF MEDICAID PAYMENTS
(For Fiscal 1971)

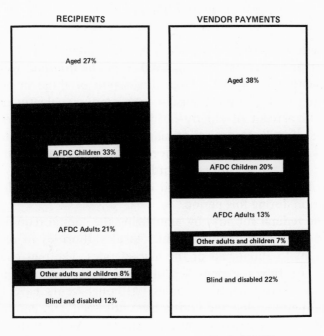

RECIPIENTS	VENDOR PAYMENTS
Aged 27%	Aged 38%
AFDC Children 33%	AFDC Children 20%
AFDC Adults 21%	AFDC Adults 13%
	Other adults and children 7%
Other adults and children 8%	Blind and disabled 22%
Blind and disabled 12%	
Total = 18 Million	Total = $5.9 Billion

Source: U.S. Department of Health, Education, and Welfare

local regulations qualify most participants in the commodity distribution program. Almost three of every four AFDC families in 1971 participated in either food stamp or donated food (commodity) plans:

Family participates	<u>73%</u>
In food stamp plan	56
In donated food plan	17
Family does not participate	<u>27</u>
In food stamp plan	20
In donated food plan	5
No food distribution in effect	2

There were some 2.5 million AFDC families in 1971, and about one in seven of them lived in public housing. Welfare recipients constituted a large proportion of those in public housing in 1969, including 44 percent of nonelderly heads and 95 percent of elderly heads of household. In 1969 the median family income of families moving into low-rent housing was $2,548, only $243 more than the median income of those who moved into such projects ten years earlier.[11] This is striking in view of the rapid rate of economic growth and inflation during this period.

The federal subsidy, by amortizing the capital required to build a housing project, enables local authorities to reduce the rent to about half of the market rates. The rent charges cover operating expenses. But these have increased more rapidly than tenants' incomes. Although rents have been raised periodically, the boosts have not been large enough to offset the increased operating expenses. As a result, local housing authorities have embarked on deficit funding and many are on the verge of bankruptcy. Nonetheless, based on the income data available, public housing authorities have apparently rejected the solution of recruiting families with higher incomes who would be able to pay rents sufficient to offset the increase in operating expenses. The federal government has also moved to subsidize maintenance costs. For example, it is authorized to pay local authorities an additional $120 per year for each family that is elderly, displaced, extremely poor, or contains four or more children. More significantly, the 1969 Housing Act further extends this supplement principle by enabling the federal government to make direct contributions to local authorities which will make up the difference between the rent needed to maintain operations and the rent that occupants can pay with one-quarter of their income. Obviously, such a program could enable families with very low incomes to become tenants in public housing without threatening the fiscal viability of these projects. It is only public housing, leased housing, and rent supplements that tend to reach families whose median incomes are around $3,500 per year.

THE IMPACT OF IN-KIND PROGRAMS

Two important problems emerge in regard to the impact of in-kind programs on work incentives. First, it is apparent that if a family receives all means-tested programs, then it will be extremely difficult for such a family ever to move off public assistance. Indeed, loss of entitlement to different in-kind programs as family earnings increase might lead to the paradoxical situation where increased earnings diminish economic well-being. But little information is available about the utilization of community resources by welfare clients, and it is uncertain how many welfare recipients are affected. Second, the more effective the efforts to recruit people for means-tested programs, the more severe will become the notch problem, where an improvement in earnings leads to a decline in the total income. Thus, to the extent that in-kind programs reach those on welfare, the more likely that the aid offered will lock them into the welfare system, inhibiting their capacity for economic self-sufficiency. This applies also to those individuals and families who do not receive cash payments but who are beneficiaries of means-tested in-kind programs. Each program establishes its own separate income threshold for eligibility, and even minimal improvements in earnings may deny the recipient entitlement to some means-tested programs. The alternative to robbing recipients of all entitlements at one swoop is to provide gradual reduction of in-kind benefits, which presents administrative difficulties. The present system avoids subjecting a family to a loss of all in-kind benefits at once.

There is no evidence that the provision of social services for welfare recipients has induced labor force participation. The principle expressed in the 1962 Social Security Amendments of pinpointing individual problems, providing counseling and guidance, and referring clients to other community institutions consumed most of the social workers' time in paper shuffling and left little for aiding clients. Not surprisingly, this produced staff frustration and accelerated turnover rates. A system designed to improve efficiency degenerated into a misallocation of scarce trained personnel and impeded the granting of emergency aid.

The failure of social services to "rehabilitate" welfare recipients led to a new emphasis on concrete programs related to employability. The emphasis shifted to day care, family planning, manpower training, and compensatory education. The expansion of legal services was an exception because it attempted to protect recipients from the arbitrary discretion of bureaucracies and to solidify rights to welfare rather than to encourage economic independence. But the effectiveness of the newer approaches in social services remains to be proved. Birth control might enhance employability, but it is not known how effectively it is used. Day care is costly; and manpower training cannot be isolated from labor market conditions.

In the wake of these experiences and frustrations, increasing emphasis is being placed upon the simplification of procedures, the separation of cash and services, and the provision of services to populations other than those on public assistance. By expanding the population served, social services tend to broaden the concepts of basic needs; but it is not at all clear whether the new strategy will also reform the individual and enhance his employability.

Since the value of the in-kind benefits available to public assistance recipients is substantial, it seems unrealistic to believe that most welfare families could secure adequate earnings to enable them to forgo these benefits. Obviously, in order to provide incentives to work and to be fully dependent on "workfare rather than welfare," the individual's earnings have to exceed the real income (including the value of in-kind services and goods) that is associated with the welfare system.

Placing a lid on eligibility for some programs and liberalizing the eligibility requirements for other programs subjects those on welfare to an extremely high marginal tax rate. Efforts to improve the efficiency and effectiveness of these in-kind programs tend only to exacerbate the problem. As the value of the in-kind programs increases, economic independence for those on welfare becomes increasingly costly, since they are subjected to a cumulative high tax rate when they raise their incomes. This will clearly become a persistent and important issue in the 1970s, because in-kind programs to meet basic necessities have in principle worked in the direction of making welfare more attractive than workfare for ever-increasing numbers.

NOTES

1. U.S. Department of Health, Education, and Welfare, *1971 Survey of Characteristics of AFDC Recipients*, Table 37.

2. Winifred Bell, "The Practical Value of Social Work Service: Preliminary Report on 10 Demonstration Projects in Public Assistance" (New York: New York School of Social Work, April 20, 1961).

3. Edward J. Mullen et al., "Preventing Chronic Welfare Dependency: An Evaluation of Public-Private Collaborative Intervention with First-Time Public Assistance Families" (New York: The Institute of Welfare Research, Community Service Society, 1970).

4. The report by the U.S. Department of Health, Education, and Welfare and the New York State Department of Social Services was printed as U.S. Congress, House Committee on Ways and Means, *Report of Findings by Special Review of Aid to Families with Dependent Children in New York City.* 91st Cong., 1st Sess. (Washington: Government Printing Office, 1969).

5. Ibid., p. 127.

6. Ludwig L. Geismar, "Thirteen Evaluative Studies in Social Work Intervention" (New Jersey: Rutgers University, 1971), unpublished paper.

7. Charles E. Gilbert, "Policy-Making in Public Welfare: The 1962 Amendments," *Political Science Quarterly* (June 1966): 196–224.

8. Rosemary Stevens and Robert Stevens, "Medicaid: Anatomy of a Dilemma," *Law and Contemporary Problems* (Spring 1970): 348–425.

9. Robert Taggart, III, *Low-Income Housing: A Critique of Federal Aid* (Baltimore, Md.: The Johns Hopkins Press, 1970), pp. 105–16.

10. Gunnar Myrdal, *Challenge to Affluence* (New York: Pantheon Books, 1963), p. 42.

11. U.S. Department of Housing and Urban Development, *Families in Low-Rent Projects* (January 1971), p. 2; and *Families Moving Into Low-Rent Housing*, October 1, 1968–September 30, 1969 (November 1970), p. 1.

3

Characteristics and Work Experience of AFDC Recipients

The distinction made by the Social Security Act between those who can support themselves and those who cannot is not based upon actual labor market operations, for work and welfare are closely intertwined.* AFDC family heads need not make an "all or nothing" choice, but may select the best combination of the two. The decision to accept welfare neither precludes participation in the labor force nor necessitates a long duration on public assistance.

THE REVOLVING DOOR

Welfare recipients are not unable or unwilling to work, nor do they languish on the rolls forever. Steady growth of the rolls masks a tremendous turnover. Some of the families who

*The National Center for Social Statistics of the U.S. Department of Health, Education, and Welfare's Social and Rehabilitation Service makes periodic surveys of AFDC recipients, gathering data on demographic, health, and financial characteristics of recipients and on program characteristics. During the last decade these surveys have been conducted in 1961, 1967, 1969, and 1971. Most of the data in this chapter are derived from these surveys.

leave the rolls later return, but there is nevertheless great dynamism in the caseload. During 1970 some 750,000 cases were closed—including nearly 40 percent of the 1.9 million AFDC households on the rolls at the beginning of the year. Thus, the 1.3 million families who received AFDC payments during all of 1970 accounted for less than one-half of the caseload at the beginning of 1971.

Most families join and leave the AFDC rolls quickly. In recent years approximately one-quarter of the cases left within six months; 30 percent left within a year; half closed within two years; and three-fifths closed within three years.

The instability of the AFDC population reflects the fact that poverty is also frequently transitory. While there was a net decline of 2 percent in the poverty population between 1965 and 1966, one-third of the poor in 1965 rose above the poverty threshold in 1966. An equal proportion of the poor in 1966 were nonpoor the previous year.[1]

The high proportion of AFDC clients who have previously received public assistance is another indication of the interdependence between work and welfare. In both 1961 and 1971 one AFDC family in three had previously received assistance. Of those in 1967 who had previously received aid, two-thirds had been on the rolls only once before and one-third had been on at least twice. Moreover, one-fifth had been denied assistance at some time.

The number of AFDC recipients mirrored national unemployment trends until the 1960s, with drops during the tight labor markets of both World War II and the Korean War. Moreover, until recently, the effect of seasonality in employment was also evident in AFDC caseloads. The greater availability of jobs during spring and summer months was reflected in slower growth or even declines in the recipient population (Chart 7).

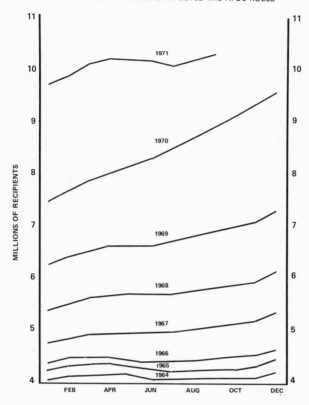

CHART 7. SEASONAL FACTORS AFFECTED THE AFDC ROLLS

Source: U.S. Department of Health, Education, and Welfare

EMPLOYABILITY OF AFDC FATHERS

Nearly one-fifth of AFDC families include a father, but two-thirds of these men are incapacitated. The others qualified for AFDC under the Unemployed Fathers (UF) component added in 1961. Only half of the states even enacted an UF component and several of these have since eliminated it.

51

These men, who worked in noncovered employment or must have exhausted their unemployment insurance and have been out of work for a substantial period of time to qualify for AFDC–UF, have been forced to rely upon welfare because of their inability to compete in the labor market. Just over one in five was a high school graduate in 1969, as contrasted with nearly three of every five adult males in the civilian labor force in 1970. About one-half of the unemployed fathers, but less than one-fifth of the civilian labor force, had failed to complete more than eight years of education (Table 5). Moreover, the unemployed fathers have few skills. Only 2 percent have never worked full time. But even among those who have been employed, only 5 percent

Table 5. AFDC unemployed fathers are poorly educated

Educational attainment (in years)	AFDC unemployed fathers, 1969	All males in the labor force 18 and over in 1970
Median	8.4	12.4
Less than 8	31%	10%
8	15	10
9 to 11	33	17
12	17	35
More than 12	4	28

SOURCE: U.S. Department of Health, Education, and Welfare, and Labor.

usually held white-collar jobs, as opposed to 47 percent nationally. Fully 64 percent were service workers or laborers, while only 13 percent of the national labor force were in these low-skilled groups (Table 6). Thus, these men are at a disadvantage in both education and skills and are usually confined to the "secondary" labor market jobs requiring few skills but offering little job stability and wages at or below the poverty level.

Table 6. AFDC unemployed fathers are concentrated in unfavorable occupations

	AFDC unemployed fathers, by current or usual occupation, 1967	Male family heads, by longest occupation during 1970
Total	100%	100%
Professional, technical, managerial	2	35
Clerical and sales	3	12
Craftsmen and operatives	30	40
Service workers	6	7
Laborers	58	7

SOURCE: U.S. Department of Health, Education, and Welfare and U.S. Bureau of the Census.

EMPLOYABILITY OF AFDC MOTHERS

As the burden of the rolls became financially onerous, public assistance for dependent children and their parents came under increasing attack. Not only was the AFDC–UF component providing support for employable male heads of families, but the role of women, especially married women, in the labor force was undergoing substantial change.

The public debate dealing with AFDC has been frequently concerned more with rhetoric than reality. The issue of whether welfare mothers *can* work has been confused with the issue of whether they *should* work and at what rate of pay. And because of the insistence that work and welfare be treated as mutually exclusive, the ability of welfare mothers to enter the labor market and earn some money has been confused with their ability to achieve economic self-support.

The original social security legislation provided assistance to mothers so that they would not be forced to work, not because they were unemployable, but because jobs were scarce. Barriers to employment, such as the physical impediments of the aged, blind, and disabled, were rare. The problem of child care, however, was and continues to be significant. Although there were few jobs available in the 1930s, even for those who sought employment, the attitude that mothers should not be forced out of the home to work prevailed into the mid-1960s.

Few married women, and especially mothers, worked prior to World War II. In 1940 only 15 percent of married women with husbands present and only 9 percent of mothers were in the work force. The succeeding three decades witnessed a continuing rise in labor force participation by women. In 1970 half of all mothers with their husbands present had work experience, including 44 percent of mothers with children under six and 58 percent of mothers with children aged six to seventeen. Exempting welfare mothers from employment when half of all mothers were working no longer seemed justified.

Though public debate continues as to whether welfare mothers should be required to work, the conclusion has generally been reached that AFDC mothers can work and should be encouraged to do so. Over the last decade, about one welfare mother in five was consistently in the labor force; moreover, the proportion in part-time work declined and that in full-time employment increased (Chart 8). A closer examination of these data reveals wide variation among states. In 1971, when 28 percent of all AFDC mothers were in the labor force or training, state rates ranged from 12 percent in Pennsylvania to 42 percent in Florida.

An examination of the characteristics of recipients suggests that for many on relief, achieving full economic independence is an unrealistic goal. However, given opportunities, suitable work incentives, and supportive services, many more

CHART 8. WORK EFFORT BY AFDC MOTHERS HAS BEEN INCREASING

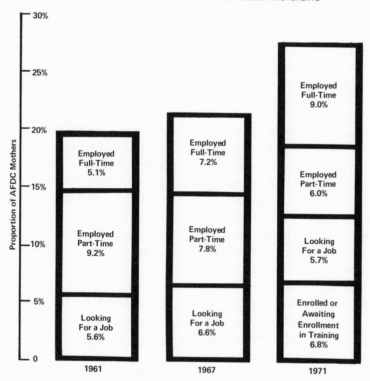

Source: U.S. Department of Health, Education, and Welfare

welfare mothers could work and earn, though these earnings could only supplement and perhaps partially substitute for public assistance, not completely replace it.

Employability is a complex balance of economic, social, and psychological factors, and attempts at precise measurement must be inconclusive. On the supply side, employability is usually associated with work experience, education, and skills, and the absence of certain barriers, including health problems, child care responsibilities, and work disincentives.

For employability and desire to work to result in a job, a demand for labor is also necessary.

Child Care

The presence of young children is the most obvious barrier to the employment of all mothers and certainly no less a problem for those on AFDC. Of all married women, husband present, with children under three, some 27 percent are in the labor force. Of AFDC women with children under three, some 14 percent are in training or at work; when the unemployed are included, the participation rate approaches 18 percent. It is increasingly acceptable for mothers to leave their children in another's care while they work. For some mothers the limited supply of day care facilities is a severe constraint, but many others have managed, nevertheless, to make arrangements.

Of every eight welfare mothers in 1971, about five had a child under six; another two had no child under six but one under thirteen; the balance had only children over thirteen. This means that more than 60 percent of the mothers might need full-time, year-round day care if they were to work; and another quarter might need care in the afternoon during the school year and all day during the summer. But according to HEW estimates, the total capacity of licensed day care centers and family day care homes in 1971 was only 750,000. In the same year there were 2.3 million AFDC children under six who presumably would need full-time care and another 2.8 million between six and twelve requiring part-time care, if their mothers were not available to care for them. Licensed facilities fell far short of being able to accommodate the children of welfare mothers. And, of course, another thirteen million working mothers might be competing for such facilities.

Nevertheless, the mothers of nearly twenty-six million minor children, including six million under six years of age, were working in March 1970.[2] These working mothers have accommodated themselves in a variety of ways to the paucity and cost of licensed facilities. The amount and types of child care arrangements used depend primarily on the number and age of the children and on the availability of relatives to provide inexpensive services. Of all employed mothers, ages thirty to forty-four, with minor children in a nationwide survey, only two in five reported the need to make regular child care arrangements; but of mothers with children under six, the proportion rose to seven in ten. Few of the mothers surveyed used facilities that might be licensed. Only one mother in eleven used a child care center. The others used, equally, relatives and nonrelatives, in either the child's or the caretaker's home. Thus, informal arrangements—which are not subject to licensing—constitute the bulk of child care.

Because preschool children must be supervised for a larger part of the day and also more carefully, daily costs rise substantially when a child under six is present (Table 7). Costs of child care also depend more heavily on the availability of relatives and others who can provide free services than on the type of services. For those who paid for child care, daily costs ranged from $2.50 to $3.50 for care by a relative, from

Table 7. Child care costs are higher for young children

	Median daily cost	
Number of children under 6	White	Black
None	$2.06	$0.70
One	3.01	1.35
Two or more	3.31	0.19[a]

[a]Apparently child care is so expensive that few black mothers with more than one preschool child work unless they can arrange for free child care.
SOURCE: Herbert Parnes et al., *Dual Careers*, Volume 1, U.S. Department of Labor, Manpower Research Monograph No. 21, 1970, p. 125.

$3.00 to more than $4.00 for care by a nonrelative, and to about $2.75 for school or group care centers. Because half of the relatives, but few of the others providing care did so without charge, the median daily costs overall were reduced to under 50 cents for care by a relative but not lowered much for other types of service. Expenditures for child care also rise with earnings. Not only can parents with higher incomes afford to spend more money, but better-paying jobs may require more reliable, more consistent, and longer care. Black mothers spend significantly less on child care than do white mothers. Not only are their incomes lower but they are also more likely to have access to relatives who will provide services without charge. Furthermore, reflecting their lower earnings, blacks are forced to choose less expensive forms of care and have lower costs for each type of child care arrangement. However, the extent to which lower costs reflect only inferior services is not known.[3]

Largely because the potential demand is so much greater than the available supply, child care has been hailed as the panacea for the employment problems of welfare mothers. Emphasizing the scarcity of child care facilities, however, may divert attention from the ability of these mothers to locate such services on their own. A woman's willingness to bear the costs of leaving her child(ren) depends largely on the expected benefits of doing so, especially on the potential earnings. A survey for the Department of Health, Education, and Welfare of AFDC in ten cities found that of all the welfare mothers sampled, two of every three "said they could make 'arrangements' (for child care) to work if a good job were available."[4]

Health

Poor health is another handicap to employment. The health problems of poor people—reinforced by inadequate diet, poor housing, and deficient medical care—are well documented. A nutrition study conducted by HEW in ten states found that persons below the poverty line were twice as likely to be low or deficient in several important nutrition criteria, including hemoglobin, that may lead to anemia.[5] A study of labor force participation in New York City poverty areas found that the incidence of disability or ill health was substantially higher than nationally. Of the population twenty-five and over, 10 percent of all men and 15 percent of all women in the poverty areas were not participating in the labor force because of health problems, as compared with 4 percent of the men and 9 percent of the women for the rest of the population.[6]

However, the impact of ill health on labor force participation by AFDC mothers is difficult to assess. About one of every nine mothers cited, in response to HEW surveys, physical or mental incapacity as the primary reason for not being in the labor force. Studies in 1968 by the Social and Rehabilitation Service indicate a higher incidence of health problems. About two mothers in five answered "yes" to the question, "Are there some kinds of jobs you can't get because of your health?" One in five answered "yes" to the question, "Does your health keep you from working altogether?"[7]

Education

The median educational attainment of welfare mothers increased between 1961 and 1971 from less than nine years to more than ten years, but still trailed by two years other adult females. The proportion who had completed eight or fewer years of schooling declined from 56 percent to 31 percent (Table 8). While education is viewed by economists as "investment in human capital" that is supposed to lead to improvement in earnings ability, the added educational

Table 8. The educational attainment of AFDC mothers has risen but still lags behind that for all women

Educational attainment (in years)	AFDC mothers		All women, 16 to 64, in the labor force, 1970
	1961	1971	
Median	8.7	10.4	12.4
Less than 8	38%	19%	6%
8	18	12	8
9 to 11	29	41	17
12	13	24	46
More than 12	2	4	24

SOURCE: Departments of Health, Education, and Welfare, and Labor.

attainment of welfare recipients does not necessarily result in rising returns. Studies have found that blacks benefit substantially less than whites from education and that in urban ghettos the returns to nonwhites are extremely small, neither increasing earnings nor decreasing unemployment.[8]

Work Experience

Reflecting the rising female participation in the labor force and the increasing interdependence of work and welfare, the work experience of AFDC mothers improved between 1961 and 1971. Although the proportion of mothers employed remained stable at about 15 percent, the proportion who had never worked dropped sharply from about one in three in 1961 to less than one in four in 1971. In addition to the mothers then working, another one-fifth had worked within the previous year and one-tenth more in the past two years. Only one mother in five had not worked at all in the last five years.

Race

The proportion of nonwhites among AFDC mothers increased substantially until the 1960s, but during the decade of greatest expansion of the rolls changed little:

	1948	1961	1971
White	69	52	52
Nonwhite	31	48	48

There is little question that blacks, chicanos, Indians, and other minority groups encounter disporportionate labor market difficulties. This discrimination is important for present purposes because these problems not only make nonwhites more likely to rely on AFDC but also decrease their ability to earn enough to escape relief.

The manifestations are many. White female family heads experience less unemployment, work in better-paying occupations, and, accordingly, are less likely to be in poverty if they are in the work force. In March 1970 almost twice as many black female family heads with minor children were unemployed as among whites. The average weekly earnings of sixteen- to forty-four-year-old female family heads in May 1969 were nearly one-fifth better for whites ($88) than for nonwhites ($74); this differential held true for all educational levels. Not only were nonwhite female family heads more likely to work in lower paying occupations, but within every occupation they were more likely to be poor. Faced with more and lengthier periods of unemployment, fewer black female family heads worked full time, year round; but more worked full time for at least half the year or part time year round. Similarly, among AFDC mothers, nonwhites are about 50 percent more likely to work than whites. For each level of labor force effort, Negroes were far more likely to be in poverty (Table 9). Thus, because of more unemployment and lower earnings for each occupation and educational level, nonwhite female family heads are about twice as likely to be poor and also about twice as likely to receive AFDC as whites.

Obviously, a group of female family heads who encounter such pervasive unfavorable conditions will be less able to earn

Table 9. Female-headed families: work experience of head, race, and poverty, 1970

	(Percent)			
	All families		Families in poverty	
	White	Negro	White	Negro
Total	100%	100%	25%	54%
With work experience	**60**	**62**	**17**	**42**
Worked at full-time job:				
50 to 52 weeks	34	27	5	18
27 to 49 weeks	8	10	17	39
26 weeks or less	6	8	50	68
Worked at part-time job:				
50 to 52 weeks	4	6	22	54
27 to 49 weeks	3	5	18	57
26 weeks or less	6	6	46	85
With no work experience	**40**	**38**	**38**	**76**

enough to avoid depending upon welfare and once they qualify for assistance to become economically self-supporting. Consequently, as the proportion of nonwhites increases, the earnings potential and capacity for self-support declines among AFDC mothers.

Demand

Even if welfare mothers were not constrained in their labor force activity by child care, health, and similar problems, their earning ability would be quite limited. Although there was some improvement between 1961 and 1971, welfare mothers are concentrated in the most unfavorable occupations and, even in comparison with all female family heads, are at a significant disadvantage. Of all AFDC mothers, 27 percent have never worked. Even those who have held jobs are concentrated in the least attractive occupations, many of them in the low-skilled, poorly-paying, transitory secondary labor market. These limited skills impede the escape of welfare mothers from poverty (Table 10).

Table 10. AFDC mothers are concentrated in low-paying jobs

	Ever-employed AFDC mothers 1967	Female family heads with work experience in 1970	
		Distribution by occupation	Proportion in poverty
Total	100%	100%	100%
Professional, technical, managerial, official	2	17	9
Clerical and sales	14	33	12
Craftsmen and operatives	12	12	46
Private household workers	20	8	56
Other service workers	28	22	34

SOURCE: U.S. Department of Health, Education, and Welfare and U.S. Bureau of the Census.

The occupational distribution of AFDC mothers will prove even more unfavorable in the future, according to projections by the Department of Labor. Their estimates suggest that welfare mothers' usual occupations are those which will increase least during the current decade. For the 27 percent of mothers who have never been employed, the shift to more highly skilled occupations is especially ominous.

Location

Fears that the suburbanization of employment would decrease employment opportunities for AFDC recipients who increasingly live in central cities may be exaggerated. It is true that employment is growing more in suburbs than in central cities and that the proportion of jobs located in suburbia is increasing. At the same time, however, central city employment has continued to grow, while population has generally stagnated, if not declined. Hence, the number of jobs per central city resident has been increasing. Moreover, there is evidence that the mix of central city employment has changed, with an increasing proportion of low-skill jobs. Thus, more of the central city jobs are within the capabilities of residents there generally, and AFDC recipients specifically. Unfortunately, low-skill jobs usually pay low wages and are not likely to be much more rewarding or remunerative than welfare.[9]

The increasing concentration of AFDC recipients in certain areas may have significant labor market implications. Such large dependence on AFDC may precipitate withdrawals from the work force, thus decreasing the supply of labor and increasing its price. Accordingly, the incomes of the working poor may increase, but this also implies a rise in production costs.

Although AFDC mothers in rural areas are slightly less likely to work than those in urban areas, participation decreases as city size grows. This is consistent with the generally more adequate benefit levels in larger industrialized areas. However, assertions that people move from the south to large northern cities in order to qualify for welfare are not well supported. A study for the House Ways and Means Committee of New York City's welfare population concluded the size of welfare payments may be a significant factor in a migrant's choice of destination, but indicated that the evidence was not adequate to assert that many recipients migrated "intentionally seeking public assistance."[10]

Work Incentives

A final consideration is the structure of work incentives. The treatment of income earned by AFDC recipients is a crucial variable in the choice between, or combination of, work and welfare. Factors reviewed above provide an indication of the extent to which welfare recipients *can* compete for employment and earnings in the labor market. But in the absence of a work requirement their decision to enter the labor force—whether they *will* compete—hinges on the incentives offered for working, which include both financial and psychological factors and can be studied from three perspectives: the relationship between work effort and existing incentives, interviews with welfare recipients and others, and the results of social experimentation.

The importance of financial incentives and alternatives to employment is underscored by the difference in labor force participation of three groups of mothers with children under three. For married women, husbands present, in this category the participation rate in 1969 was 27 percent. For other married mothers, the rate was 44 percent; after adjustments to exclude AFDC women from this group, the rate rose to about 50 percent. For AFDC mothers, the proportion either in training or at work was 18 percent. Thus, mothers of young children who have no alternative to employment are far more likely to work or seek employment than are those who can rely on a husband's income or on AFDC. Within the latter two groups, the tax bite of the AFDC women who may earn, say, $2,000 annually, including the "$30 plus one-third" disregard, is equal to the tax of other working women on an annual taxable income of over $40,000.

Despite the bias toward self-support, government policy long stifled initiative by welfare mothers. During its first three decades earnings of most AFDC recipients were treated as income available toward fulfilling predetermined needs, and assistance payments were reduced by the full amount of the earnings in the states that provided for each family the amount designated by the state as the full standard of need. This "100 percent tax" on earnings inevitably forestalled attempts to achieve financial independence. Work expenses were typically not subject to this tax. But allowing a recipient one dollar of earnings for each dollar he spent on transportation or clothes adds nothing to his disposable income and the tax robs the relief recipient of any pecuniary incentive to work. Some other states, however, paid only a proportion of the full standard. Before the 1967 amendments became effective, Indiana, for example, specified the full standard for a family of four as $287, but paid no more than $150 or 52 percent. Accordingly, the family could earn the difference of $137 without penalty, but for each additional dollar earned the welfare benefit was decreased by a dollar, constituting effectively a 100 percent tax on earnings.

States which paid less than full needs and permitted recipients to keep earnings up to the full standard provided a financial incentive to work. Public assistance recipients in these states had higher labor force participation rates than those in states that paid full needs (Table 11). But states that did not pay full needs also forced recipients to work to supplement incomes which were insufficient for subsistance living, regardless of the incentive offered.[11] About half of the welfare mothers in Alabama, Florida, and Mississippi were employed at least part of the year, because their payments were no more than 50 percent of the "basic needs" for a family of four. Southern states have also been accused of

Table 11. AFDC mothers' labor force participation was higher in states paying less than full needs, 1967

Percent of standard of needs paid	Number of states	Proportion of AFDC population	Average labor force participation rate of AFDC mothers
100	25	56%	17%
90 to 99	5	18	20
75 to 89	3	4	20
60 to 74	6	7	26
45 to 59	9	12	40
Less than 45	3	4	37

SOURCE: U.S. Department of Health, Education, and Welfare.

"encouraging" welfare recipients to do farm labor at harvest time in order not to jeopardize their eligibility for public assistance during the rest of the year and of keeping payments low to increase this leverage. This may also explain the higher employment rates in these states.[12]

There were other less significant work incentives. About half of the states allowed earnings to be retained for "future identifiable needs" of a child, such as school or health. Between 1965 and 1967 one-third of the states disregarded up to $5 a month of any income, enacted so that the increase in social security payments in 1965 would not be balanced by a decrease in public assistance. A 1965 provision allowed states to disregard earnings of teenage youth up to $50 per child or $150 per family.

The 1967 Social Security Amendments provided the first general work incentives for AFDC recipients. Whether these incentives are adequate to induce relief welfare recipients to seek employment is crucial to any contemplated design for the overhauling of AFDC.

Efforts to study work incentives have also included interviews with welfare and nonwelfare recipients. Surveys conducted by Leonard Goodwin of the Brookings Institution reveal that AFDC recipients have essentially the same attachment to the work ethic as members of families with regular workers.[13]

Social experimentation has been heralded as a basis for policymaking, and federal agencies have initiated a series of such projects in the field of income maintenance. The designs called for exploring the impact of income maintenance upon welfare recipients and working poor, whites and blacks, female-headed families and male-headed families under urban and rural settings and under a variety of benefit levels, tax rates, child care, training and other services. HEW's projects in Gary, Indiana; Seattle, Washington; Denver, Colorado;

and in rural counties in Iowa and North Carolina were started too recently to yield results yet. However, the earliest and most prominent of the projects is the Office of Economic Opportunity's much heralded New Jersey Experiment, which focuses on urban male-headed families. OEO rushed to announce that preliminary findings in early 1970 supported President Nixon's Family Assistance Plan. Their conclusions, however, may have been based more on the investigator's biases than on hard facts, and they were challenged as premature by the General Accounting Office. More recent information suggests that the experimental families' earnings have kept pace with those of the control group. Hourly earnings of experimental family heads have increased enough to compensate for a slight decline in their own hours and a larger drop in the hours worked by their wives and children. The income support apparently enabled these family heads to seek out better-paying jobs than they might have obtained in the absence of aid. Firm conclusions will not be possible until the five-year project is completed. Whether this experiment, and others begun more recently, can provide a sound basis for policy formulation remains a matter of debate.

NOTES

1. Terence F. Kelly, "Factors Affecting Poverty: A Gross Flow Analysis," in The President's Commission on Income Maintenance Programs, *Technical Studies* (Washington: Government Printing Office, 1970), p. 24.

2. U.S. Bureau of Labor Statistics, *Children of Women in the Labor Force, March 1970*, Special Labor Force Report 134, 1971.

3. Herbert Parnes et al., *Dual Careers: A Longitudinal Study of Labor Market Experience of Women*, Volume 1, U.S. Department of Labor, Manpower Research Monograph No. 21, 1970, pp. 121–27, and John R. Shea et al., *Years for Decision: A Longitudinal Study of the Educational and Labor Market Experience of Young Women*, Volume

1, Center for Human Resource Research, The Ohio State University (Columbus, Ohio, 1971), pp. 132–40.

4. Andrew K. Solarz, "Effects of Earnings Exemption Provision on AFDC Recipients," *Welfare in Review* (January–February 1971): 19.

5. Department of Health, Education, and Welfare, Public Health Service, *Ten-State Nutrition Survey in the United States, 1968–1970,* April 1971.

6. U.S. Department of Labor, Bureau of Labor Statistics, *Poverty Area Profiles: Working Age Nonparticipants: Persons Not in the Labor Force and Their Employment Problems.* Middle Atlantic Regional Report Number 22, June 1971.

7. Perry Levinson, "How Employable Are AFDC Women," *Welfare in Review* (July–August 1970): 15–16.

8. Bennett Harrison, *Education, Training and the Urban Ghetto* (Baltimore: The Johns Hopkins Press, 1972).

9. Wilfred Lewis, Jr., *Urban Growth and Suburbanization of Employment–Some New Data,* mimeographed, 1969.

10. U.S. Congress, House Committee on Ways and Means, *Report of Findings of Special Review of Aid to Families with Dependent Children in New York City,* 91st Cong., 1st Sess. (Washington: Government Printing Office, 1969), p. 35.

11. Irene Cox, "The Employment of Mothers As a Means of Family Support," *Welfare in Review* (November–December 1970): 14–15.

12. Lester M. Salamon, "Family Assistance: The Stakes in the South," *New Republic,* February 20, 1971, and Richard Armstrong, "The Looming Money Revolution Down South," *Fortune,* June 1970.

13. Leonard Goodwin, *Do the Poor Want to Work: Studies in the Work Orientation of the Poor and the Non-Poor* (Washington: Brookings Institution, 1972).

4
Work and Training

As AFDC grew steadily during the 1960s, Congress enacted a succession of programs with closely related goals to enhance the employability of welfare recipients. Even the rhetoric changed little. President Kennedy called for "rehabilitation instead of relief," and President Nixon echoed these sentiments when he urged "workfare instead of welfare." From the small Community Work and Training (CWT) program early in the decade evolved the Work Experience and Training (WET) program of the antipoverty Economic Opportunity Act. Despite a decline in national unemployment, rising governmental outlays to fight poverty, and significant reductions in the poverty population, welfare rolls grew even faster. Congress reacted with the Work Incentive (WIN) program. The underlying hope was that work would make welfare recipients "tax payers instead of tax consumers."

PRECURSORS OF WIN

"Working Off" Public Assistance

The presumption that AFDC recipients were "unemployable" and outside the work force became untenable in 1961 when the federal government extended coverage to families headed by an unemployed male parent (AFDC–UP). The need for the new law was clear: because the original Social Security Act denied assistance to families headed by an able-bodied male, the whole family was penalized if the father could not find employment. The presence of "employable" parents on relief prompted Congress in 1962 to amend the Social Security Act to subsidize employment programs for relief recipients; until 1962 all AFDC recipients were presumed to be outside the work force, and public assistance funds could not be used to provide work. States were encouraged to adopt Community Work and Training (CWT) programs designed to offer work relief rather than handouts, and hopefully also to help AFDC–UP recipients achieve economic independence.

The purpose of the amendment was twofold: to allay public criticism of relief payments to persons able to work and to create work relief projects which would train and "rehabilitate" recipients. "Working off" relief was justified as being better for the recipients' morale and providing useful public services under safeguards preventing exploitation or the displacement of regular workers. CWT's formal emphasis on training and rehabilitation reflected the nascent movement in the early 1960s toward more organized manpower and training programs for the disadvantaged.

Although the 1962 amendments were hailed as a vehicle for encouraging work and training for persons on relief, the provisions of the law tended to reinforce the more traditional "social services" associated with public assistance. Only 50–50 federal matching funds were provided for the administration of CWT projects, compared with the three-to-one ratio (75 percent federal–25 percent state) to cover the costs of social services. Project sponsors also had to contribute all of the costs of supervision, materials, and training on CWT projects, in addition to their regular matching share of public assistance. In order to obtain the maximum federal contribution, most states and localities chose therefore to expand "social services" rather than set up CWT projects.

CWT projects provided little training that would improve the employability of participants. The bulk of the funds was expended for income maintenance, leaving very little for other assistance. Nor did recipients have any monetary incentive for participating in CWT. A consistent feature of all projects, which varied considerably otherwise, was a prohibition on additional income for participants in return for work performed (other than work-connected expenses). Instead, participants were required to "work off" the amount of assistance they received, usually at the prevailing wage for comparable work performed in the community.

Antipoverty Work and Training

The Economic Opportunity Act of 1964 expanded the CWT program. Under Title V of the Act, grants were to be given to state and local welfare agencies to pay the full costs of "demonstration" projects so that the states could establish Work Experience and Training (WET) projects and provide for the expansion of CWT projects. In addition to unemployed parents on relief, "other needy persons," including single adults, were declared eligible. A 1965 amendment to the Act qualified farm families with less than $1,200 net annual income to participate in the program. But 70 percent of Title V clients were recipients of federally supported public assistance. The program reached its peak enrollment of 71,000 in 1967, divided equally between the sexes; and three of every five participants were white.

The additional funds allotted to this effort and the broadening of eligibility reflected an increasing realization that low national unemployment rates might not be suffi-

72

cient to assure a job for everyone who wants work. Even though unemployment dropped throughout the 1960s, certain groups continued to experience considerable jobless-ness. A basic tenet of the antipoverty effort was an attempt to reach out and help persons who could not compete in the labor market, in order to remove the "structural" barriers to their unemployment.

The challenge of the sponsors of Title V projects, as under CWT, was to provide useful training and work to participants. This proved to be a formidable task; most enrollees had multiple handicaps and little attachment to regular work. While the enrollees' work assignments featured a certain amount of informal vocational instruction, the bulk of these assignments was limited to low-paying, unskilled occupations. This phenomenon was understandable in light of the trainees' limited skills and educational attainment. WET project administrators, moreover, advanced little evidence that occupational training led to the upgrading of trainees over their former occupational levels or that Title V training led to more advanced vocational education.

Title V administrators did not make adequate use of the flexibility they had in utilizing funds. Individual employ-ability plans provided for a combination of vocational training, work experience, education, and day care; but these existed more in the rhetoric of WET officials than in project implementation. Private employers were for all practical purposes ignored by Title V administrators, and emphasis was placed on complex "rehabilitative" services or work experi-ence even though assistance alone, for example, might have helped the client. Whatever the rhetoric used, the welfare agencies responsible for the administration of Title V projects found it difficult to expand their activities beyond traditional income support efforts. With little or no prior experience with training or placement, or awareness of labor market operations, the state and local welfare agencies were hard put to design work experience projects which would enhance the employability and earning potential of enrollees.

Despite laudable goals of rehabilitation and uplift, WET remained primarily a work relief and income maintenance program. Expenditure patterns show this clearly: in fiscal 1968, for example, well over one-half of the $1,368 average cost per enrollee was spent for income maintenance, but only one-sixth each for work experience activities and vocational education.

The overall success of WET in reducing dependency through rehabilitation was modest. According to one survey, three of every four trainees departed without completing their assignments; only one-fifth of them left to take a job. Half of the trainees who left Title V (whether by "graduation" or drop out) continued on public assistance rolls; of these, only 17 percent were employed.[1]

Nor did "graduation" presage success. Of the 42,000 trainees completing all training prescribed for them during the first three years of the program, one-half obtained employment immediately; another one-eighth went on to advanced training under other programs; and fully three-eighths were unable to find employment immediately following completion of their Title V training. Indeed there is little evidence that the employability of participants improved, since the average family with an employable father remains on relief for less than a year and thus most would have found employment even without the program in the tight labor market that prevailed during the life of the WET program.

1967 SOCIAL SECURITY AMENDMENTS

The poor record of WET did not discourage Congress from further attempts to induce welfare recipients to seek work.

Perhaps the best indicator of Congress' jaundiced view of welfare was the 1967 attempt to "freeze" the AFDC rolls. The "freeze" was repealed before going into effect, but the efforts to improve the employability of welfare recipients persevered under the Work Incentive (WIN) program of 1967, signed by the President in January 1968.

WIN was designed to do gradually what the freeze would have done abruptly—stop the growth of welfare and then reverse the trend. Changes from WET in target, stewardship, and methods reflected the new focus. While WET had been part of an overall antipoverty effort, WIN was focused exclusively on relief recipients. Under WET the Labor Department supplied manpower services and the Department of Health, Education, and Welfare retained responsibility for all other activities. In WIN the Labor Department had responsibility for training and employment, while HEW screened and referred enrollees and provided supportive services. HEW's intention in WET to "rehabilitate" relief recipients by improving their total environment had produced too few results. Labor was expected to focus more clearly on employability.

Conceptually, WIN went far beyond WET in attempting to allow AFDC recipients to "become wage-earning members of society and restore their families to independent and useful roles in their communities."[2] WIN's tools also reflected the new purpose. All enrollees in training would receive monthly payments for participation and, for the first time, general work incentives would be provided in the form of earnings exemptions. There was also a work requirement for able-bodied fathers in those states with an UF component, out-of-school youths sixteen or over, and other adults besides parents. Services after enrollment were again designed more clearly to lead to jobs. As under WET, an "employability plan" for each enrollee was to outline his path to employment. In addition to WIN's own components, moreover, all existing manpower programs could be utilized. Finally, follow-up services were to be provided for three to six months; and an enrollee must have continued in employment throughout that period to be considered a "graduate."

Hopes ran high. HEW, whose experience with WET should have dampened enthusiasm for the new effort, painted a particularly glowing picture of WIN's promise. Spokesmen for the department estimated that some 900,000 individuals and their families might work their way off welfare between 1969 and 1974. At the same time, other HEW officials were considerably underestimating to Congress continued increases in the AFDC rolls. The Labor Department, which had far more experience in the manpower field was less enthusiastic but nevertheless optimistic, projecting that a total of 240,000 persons could be placed in employment between 1969 and 1972.[3]

Lofty hopes for WIN remained an article of faith, or possibly habit, with high administration officials, even in the face of disappointing performance. Although WIN became mandatory in all states only in mid-1969 and enrollment was 64,000 in August 1969, former Labor Secretary George Shultz estimated in October 1969 that enrollment would reach 150,000 by the end of fiscal 1970. Actual enrollment as of June 30, 1970 was about 95,000. Even by the end of fiscal 1971—a full year later—enrollment was 109,000. And enrollment in WIN should by no means be equated with training or preparation for economic independence.

IDENTIFYING ENROLLEES FOR WIN

HEW's duties under WIN were restricted to the department's areas of expertise. Removed from designing or operating manpower components, HEW retained responsibility for screening AFDC recipients and referring them to WIN, for continuing assistance payments, and for providing supportive services. According to Labor's guidelines, the public employment service (ES) offices funded by the Department of Labor were to take the individuals referred by the local welfare agency and "move [them] through an experience of work, training, and education . . . [to] employment with a future."

The number of potential enrollees in WIN far exceeded the number of slots. Despite WIN's lofty long-range goal of "restoring to economic independence *all* employable persons of 16 and over in AFDC families,"[4] aspirations had to be tempered by the availability of resources. In 1967, for example, there were more than 2.2 million adults and children sixteen or over in AFDC families, including 1,120,000 mothers or stepmothers and 240,000 father or stepfathers. Many of these parents and other adults were handicapped or disabled, and the task of assessing the employability of so many persons and providing manpower services was massive. Accordingly, a priority system was established to govern their screening and referral.

The legislation identified groups of recipients who could be referred to WIN and exempted others. Among individuals found "appropriate," unemployed fathers were to be referred first—within thirty days of receipt of assistance. Except for unemployed fathers, assessments were to be conducted on a first-come, first-served basis. Other "mandatory" referrals were to be dependent youths, and other persons whose needs are counted in determining benefits, who were sixteen or over and who were not substantially full-time in school, at work, or in training and not expecting to continue education within three months. In addition to these groups, states were allowed to establish other mandatory groups. Other categories of recipients could volunteer for WIN, provided that their participation was not inimical to the person's or family's welfare.

Persons could not be referred who were: (1) ill, incapacitated, or aged; (2) too remote from any WIN project to participate effectively; (3) attending school full-time or expecting to do so within three months; (4) required in the home on a substantially continuous basis because of the illness or incapacity of another household member; or (5) lacking adequate child-care arrangements.

After a federal judge in Washington state ruled that the "male priority" clause discriminated against women, HEW prepared to eliminate all priorities for referral and enrollment. But amendments passed in December 1971 essentially reaffirmed the "male priority."

In addition to determining each AFDC adult recipient's appropriateness in accordance with these criteria, state welfare agencies were required to provide various prereferral services. Each person considered for referral was to receive careful explanation of the WIN program, the rights and responsibilities of a participant, financial changes, and related matters; a medical examination was required unless such information was available and current; adequate child care services were to be provided each referral; transportation was to be arranged if not available; and family planning services were to be made available where appropriate. After the necessary conditions were met, the appropriate individuals could be referred to WIN in the order stated. After referring an individual to the state employment service for training or employment, the local welfare agency continued its responsibility for child care and family planning services and for disbursing appropriate assistance payments.

Referrals from the welfare agency are again assessed by the manpower agency and "inappropriate referrals" are returned. The priority system prescribed for referring individuals to

WIN was supposed to result in "creaming" of the entire population. Selecting first AFDC fathers, then mothers who had already been enrolled in training meant that the earliest WIN enrollees would be disproportionately males with work experience and those females who apparently had no significant barriers to training. The proportion of females and nonwhites increased until the onslaught of the recession. By the time WIN became fully operative in fiscal 1971, nearly two of every five enrollees were males and more than half of the enrollees were white (Chart 9).

INCENTIVES

The realization that welfare recipients, like everyone else, would be spurred to enter training or employment by mone-

CHART 9. WIN ENROLLEES ARE BECOMING BETTER EDUCATED
(Data for Fiscal Years)

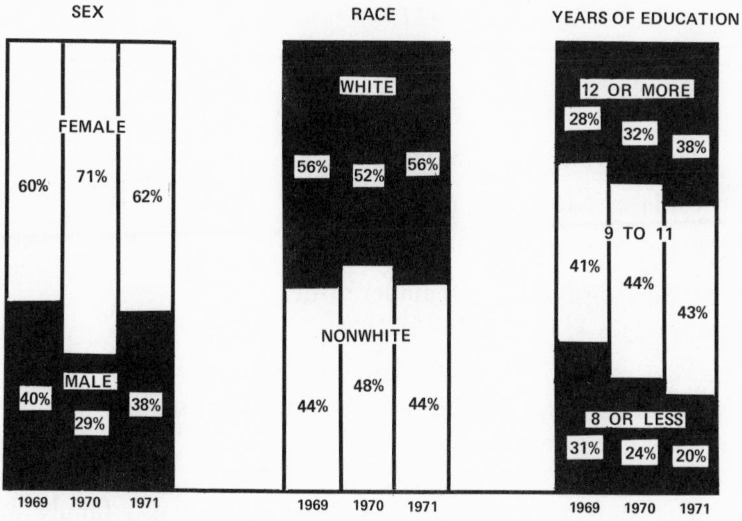

Source: U.S. Department of Labor

tary incentives was incorporated into the 1967 Social
Security Amendments. Previously, as noted in Chapter 3,
welfare payments in many states were reduced dollar for
dollar as earnings increased. The amendments provided that
$30 and one-third of the remainder plus work expenses be
disregarded in computing each month's benefit. The tax rate
implicit in the "$30 and 1/3" disregard was steep, subjecting
net earnings above $30 to a tax rate of 67 percent, applicable
to the general populace only at incomes above $140,000.
However, a state's interpretation and calculation of the disregard can considerably soften the tax bite, according to GAO's
illustration of a working mother with three children—two of
whom require child care—in Los Angeles:[5]

The monthly earnings of an AFDC mother in Los Angeles working full time at $2.50 per hour amounted to		$433
Less payroll deductions		-54
Leaving her net take-home pay of		379
Less work-related expenses		-212
Standard allowance for food and incidentals	$25	
Transportation, including car maintenance	80	
Child care for two children	107	
The statutory disregard is		-30
Plus one-third of the remainder of her gross wages 1/3 × (433-$30)		-134
Her net pay for computation of supplemental benefits, after subtracting work-related expenses and income disregards, is		$ 3

The state of California has determined that a family of
four has monthly "needs" of $285, but pays no more than

$221. For this mother the supplemental benefit equals the difference between her level of needs ($285) and her "net" pay ($3), up to the limit of $221. If the state provided the full amount of "needs" she would receive $282.

This method, however, allows double counting a portion of payroll deductions and work expenses. A less generous computation but possibly more in keeping with the spirit of the legislation would allow her the same payroll deductions and work-related expenses, but calculate the income disregard on the basis of her net pay after these expenses, not on the basis of her gross wages. Thus, her income exclusion would not be $164, or $30 plus 1/3 times ($433–$30), but only $76, or $30 + 1/3 × ($433–$54–$212–$30). Her net pay for computing her welfare supplemental would be $91, instead of $3, and her supplemental, $194, instead of $221. Furthermore, if California met fully its standard of needs, she would still get $194, instead of $282.

This example demonstrates why so few AFDC recipients work their way off welfare. HEW's method of computation substantially increases the amount of supplemental benefits paid and allows to remain on AFDC families who would otherwise cease to qualify, thus enlarging welfare rolls.

The example also shows that calculating the benefits of working is no simple exercise. A survey of welfare mothers in California found that "few of the mothers had any clear idea whether, by going to work, they would be increasing their incomes a little, a lot, or not at all." This is hardly surprising, because such calculations are "confounded by allowances for work expenses (to a considerable extent at the discretion of the individual caseworker, who often changes from month to month), by changing family composition, shifting amounts of other income (e.g., husband's income, child support payments), adjustments for overpayment or underpayment in prior months, the hard-to-quantify value of medical care and food stamps, and so forth."[6]

At least as important as the complexity of calculations is knowledge that these incentives exist. Information about the new policy, however, has not been widely disseminated. Interviews conducted in ten major cities in 1970 revealed that only one-sixth of AFDC family heads were aware of the new policy even six months after it went into effect.[7]

Still another flaw in the incentive system is the different treatment of male and female family heads. Supplemental benefits for the latter are computed as explained above, regardless of hours worked, on gross income and associated costs. This procedure applies to males if they work less than 100 hours per month. If they work more, they are automatically excluded from the welfare rolls, regardless of earnings and this may inhibit their work effort, thus barring them from many steady and probably better paying jobs and confining them to less regular and less remunerative employment. For many men, even full-time work may yield less income than assistance alone. The GAO found that in Los Angeles the average father actually lost $65 per month by accepting full-time employment.

WIN COMPONENTS

The local employment service office assesses referrals from the local welfare agency in the order of their referral. Individuals deemed unsuitable for training or employment are returned to the local welfare agency after consultation and all others are classified into three groups on the basis of job-readiness: Priority I, placement in a job or in on-the-job training; Priority II, placement in work experience and/or institutional training; and Priority III, placement in public service employment for persons not able to be placed in regular jobs or benefit substantially from training.

The Design

Each enrollee is assigned to an "employability team," including a counselor and a work and training specialist. This team was to devise for each enrollee, and re-evaluate continually, an "employability plan" or "blueprint" to provide "direction and continuity without rigidity in the movement of enrollees through the WIN program into a job," according to Labor Department guidelines, which provides "a reasonable prospect of self-sufficiency," defined ordinarily as wages of at least $1.60 per hour.

No stops were to be spared to enable enrollees to forsake relief rolls through training and employment. The design and rhetoric provided for diverse options. All enrollees not immediately placed in employment or in another program would receive up to four weeks' orientation to the WIN program and to the "world of work." Many enrollees were expected to require educational services. These could be provided by subcontracting to accredited training institutions, both public and private, or by hiring qualified staff. Because of its importance to employment success, education would be provided prior to or concurrently with work experience or training. No predetermined minimum attainment was prescribed; rather, the enrollees' achievement depended on his abilities and goals. A wide variety of work and training components were to be made available, including on-the-job training, provided the employer has indicated he intends to retain the individual after successful completion of training; institutional training, with an emphasis on classroom vocational education and workshop training; paraprofessional training, geared to entry-level jobs with "realistic career ladders" in public service fields; work experience, to be provided by public or private nonprofit agencies to allow development of basic work habits, exploration of various occupational fields, and gaining knowledge of the "world of work," rather than on developing an occupational skill; and public service employment in unskilled or low-skilled jobs as long as was needed, but with re-evaluation every three months, for persons unable either to find jobs in the regular economy or to benefit from work experience or training.

When appropriate jobs were not available, the local ES was to solicit and develop openings with employers and also work with employers and unions in restructuring staffing patterns ("job engineering"). And if jobs could not be developed in the enrollee's labor market, the local employment service could subsidize relocation. Once placed in a job, an enrollee was to receive supportive services for at least 90 days but generally not over 180 days. Only those enrollees who had successfully completed the follow-up period while regularly employed were to be considered "graduates." This unusually stringent operational definition was consistent with WIN's stress on thoroughness and stated aim of providing training leading to employment.

As might be expected, WIN's implementation did not conform exactly to this elaborate design. Training slots were not always available and program administrators could not promise a job and economic independence to the most cooperative trainees. Nor did enrollment in WIN necessarily guarantee training. Of WIN enrollees in mid-1970 and late 1971, about half were actually receiving education or training and one in seven was at work and receiving supportive services, but one in twelve was being processed into the program and one in four was nominally enrolled but not assigned to work or preparation for work (Table 12).

Training

Institutional training accounts for the bulk of WIN training. The choice of occupations for which enrollees are trained

Table 12. WIN enrollment by component

Component	April 1970	September 1971
TOTAL	89,445	117,409
	100%	100%
Working, and receiving supportive services	14	14
Orientation and assessment	7	8
Education, training, experience	54	51
Education	22	16
Training	26	26
Work experience	2	4
Other training programs	5	6
Waiting	25	27

SOURCE: U.S. Department of Labor.

is determined at the local level, where the employment service's knowledge of specific job market conditions is presumably most adequate to guide the WIN team.

A wide variety of occupations is included, although in no project would an enrollee have so great a choice. Furthermore, the sex composition of WIN trainees largely determines the occupational mix. Nearly three-quarters of the training planned by WIN for fiscal 1971 and 1972 was in paraprofessional, clerical, sales, and services occupations dominated by women. Blue-collar occupations, which are filled primarily by men, accounted for only one-quarter of the training (Table 13).

Next to direct placement in a job, the most favorable component is on-the-job training (OJT), because the enrollee must function in a regular work situation, receives wages, and—if he successfully completes the training period—is likely to be hired as a regular employee. Reimbursement to employers ranges from an average of $700 per trainee to cover excessive wastage of materials and the necessary increase in supervision and training to reimbursement for a wide range of services, including supervision, remedial education counsel-

Table 13. Institutional training under WIN in fiscal 1971 and 1972

Occupational class	
TOTAL	*100%*
Professional, technical	10
Clerical and sales	41
Service	23
Processing	4
Machine trades	3
Bench work	6
Structural work	9
Miscellaneous	4

SOURCE: U.S. Department of Labor.

ing, and vocational training at an average cost of $3,500 per trainee. OJT has expanded slowly from under 300 at the beginning of fiscal 1970 to about 3,000 by the end of fiscal 1971, including WIN enrollees transferred to JOBS. According to the Labor Department, the underutilization of OJT was due to foot-dragging by the states that generally inhibit use of OJT and impose time-consuming processes for contract approval when OJT is tried. Predictably, states have attempted to place part of the burden for OJT's slow growth on the federal government.

Finally, a limitation on OJT over which neither the federal nor local manpower authorities have much control is national economic softness. In loose labor markets, when many skilled and experienced persons are seeking work, programs to upgrade the disadvantaged can have little success. This tenet of manpower planning was graphically illustrated in the JOBS program recently, where terminations increased and hires decreased as national unemployment rose.

In late 1971 the Labor Department decided to reemphasize OJT, using the JOBS optional program format, appealing to small employers rather than only to large corporations. Furthermore, to counter the scarcity of positions in the private sector, the 1971 Social Security Amendments ear-marked one-third of WIN expenditures beginning in fiscal 1973 for OJT or public service employment. Finally, a provision of the Revenue Act of 1971 permits employers to deduct from their taxable income 20 percent of the wages, including those for OJT, paid to WIN participants during their first year of employment. The annual cost of this credit has been estimated at $25 million.

Public Service Employment

So-called "special work projects" loomed large in the earliest plans for WIN to assist "persons without immediate jobs or training prospects." In 1969 fully one-fifth of 1969's WIN enrollees were to be assigned to special work projects. But enthusiasm declined rapidly and participation in 1971 accounted for only 1 percent of WIN enrollment. As originally envisioned by Congress, special work projects called for the Secretary of Labor to find for Priority III individuals work opportunities with public or private nonprofit employers. The individual would be paid directly by the employer—receiving a paycheck rather than a welfare check was one of the program's selling points. The implementation was never developed. It is not surprising that some equated special work projects with make-work projects; one Congressman referred to the effort as "a WPA project with Rube Goldberg financing."

An examination of the financing suggests that the program was not taken seriously despite all the rhetoric. At least 20 percent of the cost was to be borne by the employer. Complicated financial arrangements between the local manpower and welfare agencies were required, and there was little federal money to get the projects started. Moreover, the program offered little incentive to the enrollee. Instead of a relief check, he would receive a paycheck directly from the employer which equaled his maintenance grant plus 20 percent of his wage—which meant that his gross income was certainly increased. However, his payments from the employer were "true wages," subject to social security and income taxes, which were likely to eat up most of the 20 percent added to his maintenance grant. It is not surprising, therefore, that the component was little utilized. By the end of fiscal 1971, enrollment had inched to only 1,150. An amendment in late 1971, however, rechristened the projects as "public service employment," provided generous federal participation, and, as noted above, earmarked substantial funds for their implementation.

Other Manpower Programs

WIN's flexibility is enhanced by the ability to transfer enrollees to other suitable manpower programs. However, only 6 percent of WIN enrollees have been tranferred to MDTA, JOBS, and other training programs administered by the Labor Department. Nevertheless, a substantial number of AFDC recipients have enrolled directly in manpower programs. Public assistance recipients accounted in fiscal 1971 for about 15 percent of the enrollees in "adult" Labor Department efforts, including 16 percent in MDTA–Institutional, 5 percent in MDTA–OJT, 14 percent in CEP, and 16 percent in JOBS. In addition, almost 290,000 youths from welfare families constituted over one-third of the Neighborhood Youth Corps and Job Corps enrollments.

Relocation

Although the law provides for funding the relocation of welfare recipients, WIN used it very sparingly and is reminiscent of the mother in the folk song that allows her daughter to go swimming but admonishes her not to get wet. WIN's meager use of relocation stems both from the stringent wording of the relevant portion of the 1967 amendments and from Labor Department actions. The legislation imposed requirements for relocation which were much tougher than the goals of other WIN activities. The Labor Department created other roadblocks by taking more than two years to issue guidelines on relocation and by limiting average costs to $360, including per diem assistance of only $20 per day for a family of four for no more than five days.

Through the end of fiscal 1971, fewer than 700 enrollees had received relocation assistance, many of them from West Virginia. Even though the 1971 amendments relaxed relocation provisions, relocation involves an inordinate amount of effort by the WIN staff and is not likely to be encouraged by them.

Waiting

After being accepted into WIN, a person is considered enrolled until he terminates either by completing training and follow-up or by leaving with or without good cause before that. Hence, enrollment continues even during inactive periods. These may occur before he is placed in an initial component; between components, when requirements of the individually tailored employability plan do not dovetail with available training; during training, when personal emergencies require attention; and between completion of training and job placement.

Waiting, or holding, has continued to account for a substantial proportion of all WIN enrollees—27 percent in late 1971. However, the composition of holding has changed considerably and these trends reflect the maturation of WIN. In the program's infancy, when referrals from the welfare agency exceeded the manpower agencies' training capacity, holding at the beginning of the WIN process—at intake—accounted for 29 percent; at the end of WIN, persons who had finished training and were waiting for jobs accounted for only 7 percent, in part because relatively few enrollees had completed training and because placements for them were easier. By late 1971 the manpower agencies apparently were able to keep up with referrals and holding at intake was down to 17 percent; but WIN's ability to arrange training was frustrated because the job market was unable to absorb enrollees as fast as they completed training and job entry waiting had jumped to 29 percent. Also evident is a marked increase in the number of enrollees who have temporarily left the program because of personal problems and a decrease in the proportion waiting to continue training (Table 14).

Table 14. Waiting in WIN, 1970 and 1971

	May, 1970	September 1971
Number in waiting	24,771	31,518
Proportion of WIN enrollees	27%	27%
TOTAL	100%	100%
Intake phase	29	17
Program related	55	30
Nonprogram related	9	23
Job entry	7	30

SOURCE: U.S. Department of Labor.

The rapid growth in the number of persons waiting for a job highlights WIN's inability to place enrollees, because the number at work and receiving follow-up services has not increased as fast as job entry holding. In May 1970 there was only one person waiting for a job (who could have been working) for every six persons at work in follow-up. By September 1971 there was more than one person who could have been working for every three persons who were in jobs.

CHILD CARE AND FAMILY PLANNING

The role of child care in allowing mothers to participate in training and employment is crucial for the WIN program. The proportion of mothers found inappropriate for referral because they lack appropriate child care services and the proportion of mothers who dropped out of training for the same reason demonstrated again the significance of this supportive service. And the difficulties experienced by HEW and the local welfare agencies in remedying this problem have significantly hampered the WIN program, because no mother can be referred to WIN unless her children will receive "adequate" day care. In the early days of WIN, former HEW Secretary Robert Finch said, "the failure of day care in great part has contributed to the failure of the WIN program."[8]

A wide variety of child care arrangements are being used. Despite an increasing emphasis on organized and licensed day care facilities, there has been little change in the proportion of children receiving care at home. By the middle of 1971, over 100,000 children were receiving WIN child care, 46 percent in their own home and 54 percent outside their home, at a relative's home, day care facility, or other arrangements:

Own home	Relative's home	Day care facility	Other
46	10	23	24

Children up to fourteen are eligible to receive care, but care for children under three is frowned upon. Of the children receiving care at the end of 1970, nearly two-thirds were preschool children, while the other third were school age. The proportion of children under six has been increasing.

Working mothers are supposed to contribute to the costs of child care. But realizing that WIN graduates were not

91

likely to secure wages adequate to cover all child care costs, HEW was prepared for lengthy participation. "The majority of WIN mothers," according to testimony presented by HEW before the House Appropriations Committee, "require child care when they enter WIN, and child care would be required for 2 to 3 years following initial enrollment in WIN."[9] And a year later that view was reinforced: "Some mothers will require child care indefinitely, especially those with more than one child who requires care."[10]

Not only mothers currently enrolled in WIN but working graduates of the program are eligible for child care. However, because enrollees have not found employment as quickly as expected and initial enrollments have continued, working mothers' offspring constituted only about 15 percent of the WIN child care population.

WIN's problems in providing day care extend beyond the critical national shortage of day care facilities. No federal funds were provided for acquiring or constructing facilities and the state welfare agencies must supply one of every four dollars. Even though a number of states planned to use Model Cities funds from the Department of Housing and Urban Development as the state share, raising the nonfederal 25 percent was a mammoth job.

Local welfare agencies, already taxed by rising caseloads, high staff turnover, and inexperienced personnel, received no additional manpower for their new duties under WIN; nor were their caseworkers knowledgeable about child care. Finally, the potential supply of facilities was reduced and their cost increased by strict federal standards that were difficult to implement within realistic budgetary constraints. Indeed, it has been suggested that very few children of middle-class parents receive the comprehensive care prescribed by federal standards. In actual practice, the facilities provided fell short of the guideline models but still added appreciably to WIN's costs. In mid-1971 annual day care costs ranged from $879 at home to $1,163 in day care centers. A relaxation of the expensive federal standards can be expected to conform to realistic market conditions.[11]

Whatever the costs, there are strong indications that child care will be expanded in the foreseeable future. The House-approved H.R. 1 included an annual $750 million authorization for child care services and Congress approved in 1971 a bill that would have expended nearly three times as much to provide not only for children of working welfare recipients but also for children of the near poor. President Nixon vetoed this bill, but support for child care continues to gain momentum.

Congress deemed family planning services so important that the 1967 amendments earmarked 6 percent of the social services funds for that purpose. Not only do additional children increase the income level needed to escape poverty but pregnancy and additional child problems often hinder and sometimes force withdrawal from training and employment. Indeed, of all women terminated for good cause in fiscal 1970, one in ten listed pregnancy as the cause of termination. Various services are provided by local welfare agencies under Maternal and Child Health programs, depending on the state. Information and referral services are available in all states but one; counseling, in all but eight; services from physicians and/or clinics and supplies can be purchased in all but fourteen.

THE *WIN* FUNNEL

Cumulatively through fiscal 1971, a total of 2.7 million assessments of AFDC recipients had been completed. Only 24 percent of the assessees were deemed "appropriate for referral" to WIN. The proportion found appropriate varied considerably among states ranging from two-thirds or more in nine states to less than one-third in nineteen. The reasons individuals were found inappropriate reflect the barriers to employment faced by AFDC recipients. Of 186,000 assessed in the second quarter of 1971, for example, only 56,000 were found appropriate. The others were disqualified for a variety of reasons:

Total	100%
Required in home because of age or number of children	28
Illness, disability, or advanced age	22
Child aged 16–20 attending school full time	7
Adequate child care arrangements not currently available	7
Currently receiving or referred to vocational rehabilitation or other education or training	5
Required in home because of illness or incapcity of other member of household	3
Remoteness from WIN projects	2
Other	26

These reasons varied between states. Remoteness was a greater problem in Alaska and Arizona than in New Jersey and Pennsylvania, while lack of child care was more common in Illinois and New York than in Mississippi and Tennessee. This initial stage of the "funnel" is necessary to weed out persons with obvious problems, thus identifying the more employable among AFDC recipients.

Leaks at later stages are crucial to program success. The first of these leaks is between assessment and referral. Of 627,000 persons found appropriate for referral through June 1971, only 79 percent were actually referred. Of 493,000 actually referred to WIN, fewer than three of five actually enrolled. A variety of reasons account for this slippage, which was reduced but still constituted one-third of all referrals during fiscal 1971. According to Labor Department data, 13 percent of those not enrolled were immediately referred back to the welfare agency as unsuitable or because slots were not open; 12 percent failed to attend scheduled interviews; and 8 percent were interviewed and found not acceptable. HEW data indicate that nearly one in ten was referred back because of refusal "without good cause to accept work or training."

The widespread failure to enroll indicates flaws in program administration: that referred individuals choose not to enroll casts doubts on the attractiveness of WIN and on the motivation of AFDC recipients; that referred individuals cannot be accommodated in programs indicates inadequate coordination between local welfare and manpower units and results in unnecessary paperwork and frustration among referred persons; that they are not suitable for enrollment reflects the lack of workable guidelines or adherence to them.

Recipients are allowed to contest referral to WIN. However, the sanctions provided for those who refuse to participate in the program have been more bark than bite. A General Accounting Office (GAO) study concluded that the effectiveness of existing sanctions is questionable. Not only are local agencies reluctant about enforcement, but the provisions have few teeth in any case. The GAO found that an AFDC father's refusal to participate would cost his family only $19 per month in Los Angeles or $50 per month in Denver. In addition, the welfare agency can withhold about half of the family's assistance payment to pay directly certain expenses. When the state makes these "vendor payments," it ensures that the family's needs are met but reduces the amount of money the family controls—certainly a mild sanction. Welfare agencies have hesitated to apply even these measures because they might impose financial hardship on the family, create family tension, bring pressure on the father to leave, and require tedious clerical work for the agency.

95

The GAO found in the above study that in Denver not a single family payment had been reduced, although ninety-four men had refused to participate; in only six cases had vendor payments been arranged. And in Los Angeles, in cases where payments had actually been reduced only 7 percent of the men subsequently enrolled.[12]

Whatever the reasons for leakages between referral and enrollment, the wholesale over-referral to the manpower agencies creates unnecessary paperwork. This hinders the effectiveness of both agencies in providing services and is likely to result in frustration and bitterness as recipients are shuttled between welfare and manpower agencies.

Enrollment in WIN is no guarantee of success. A large proportion of enrollees leave before completing their employability plan and irregular attendance is common.

Participation in WIN is largely a function of the positive and negative sanctions. Though participation is mandatory for able-bodied fathers and out-of-school youths aged sixteen and over, the GAO study found that at least in Los Angeles and Denver local welfare officials were unwilling or unable to require fathers to participate. The Olympus Research Corporation found a similar lack of participation by youths in the Boston program.[13] Although participation has been made mandatory in some states for mothers with suitable child care arrangements, in most states mothers participate only voluntarily, and therefore are free to leave without penalty. Thus, sanctions are not generally effective, even when applied, against fathers, youths, and others, who comprise less than half of WIN enrollment. Mothers constitute over half of WIN enrollment, but no sanctions are provided against most of them.

Positive incentives for participation may be little more promising. A monthly allowance of $30 plus transportation and work expenses is provided for participants during intake, education, and institutional training. While this additional compensation is an improvement over earlier programs, even welfare recipients may not find $1.50 a day an adequate incentive. Furthermore, enrollees in "holding" can receive the allowance for only one month, even though four enrollees in five spend more time in this component—the mean duration is almost four months.

Lacking effective sanctions either in requirements or allowances for participation, WIN must rely primarily on the promise that training will lead to employment to promote attendance. If program retention and attendance reflect program effectiveness, then WIN fails the test. Of 200,000 who had left the program—out of a total enrollment of 317,000 through September 1971—only one of every five completed the course of training. Reasons for termination included health and pregnancy, moving from the area, family care, leaving welfare rolls, and refusal to continue with training (Table 15). Even after job entry, attrition was substantial; of nearly 50,000 placed in jobs between July 1970 and

Table 15. "Good Cause" terminations from WIN

Total	100%
Health	20
Family care required	14
Moved	12
Voluntary withdrawal by mothers	12
No longer on welfare	9
Pregnancy	6
Found own job	3
Referred in error	3
Institutionalized	2
Armed forces and schooling	2
No suitable training	2
Unknown	13

SOURCE: Analytic Systems Inc., *Analysis of WIN Program Termination Data, Fiscal Year 1970.*

September 1971, only 27,000 remained employed for six months.

Although specific data are not available, attendance is often a problem. Transportation, for example, is particularly troublesome in rural areas, while child care and health problems are universal. Absence for these reasons may be perfectly valid, but suggestions that valid absences are not cause for concern are misguided. Measures like mobile classrooms and buses for trainees, and better child care and medical service during training are essentially palliative, for the problems they address are not likely to be "solved." Unless employment leads to substantially higher earnings, reliance on public or undependable private transportation will continue after employment, as will child care and health difficulties. Hence, these "valid" reasons for nonattendance may portend little more success than willful absence. Other reasons are frequently due to chance occurrences, like the theft of a welfare check or condemnation of a dwelling.

There is no need to determine the immediate reasons for absenteeism because they reflect problems basic to WIN. The facts, briefly, are: few good jobs are accessible to graduates; hence, placement rates are low; monetary incentives for training are weak; this paucity of tangible rewards for training is reflected in low attendance rates; the quality of training certainly suffers from sporadic attendance; when placements are scarce for well-trained enrollees, they must be even less plentiful for enrollees with mediocre attendance and training records. Thus, like the chicken and the egg, poor attendance and low program success are inseparable.

Two approaches concerning attendance are prominent among WIN staff. The hardliners would authorize special rewards for attendance and sanctions for absenteeism. The softliners question the effect of sticks or carrots tied to attendance and tend to emphasize the availability of good jobs at the end of the line. Tougher sanctions would undoubtedly spur attendance, but what point is there in forcing enrollees to attend training? Requiring public assistance recipients to "work off" their grants was a primary rationale for CWT and may still be valid, but it is more appropriate for work projects than for training. Attempting to change recipients' behavior by training them for jobs was important in WET and paramount in WIN. But when enrollment is unlikely to lead to jobs, what justification is there for training requirements. If the program is weak, there is little point in requiring attendance. If the training is effective, it would attract trainees seeking economic independence and those that can be motivated. In the words of an ES official, "if our program is vital, attendance will in many cases take care of itself." This line of reasoning—that the resources used in keeping track of attendance and counseling absentees can be redirected to increase program effectiveness—is worth serious consideration. Indeed, unless WIN is to be only a punishment for AFDC recipients, the primary emphasis must be on program effectiveness, thus creating an incentive for training.

Of all persons leaving WIN through September 1971, only 22 percent had completed training and remained employed during the three- to six-month follow-up period. But a sampling of those who had successfully completed the follow-up period found that 80 percent were employed six months later. That so many graduates were employed a year after placement presumably indicates effectiveness at the final stage of the WIN funnel. But considering the high selectivity of those who reach the end of the line, the gratifying results must be balanced against the high costs of the total effort.

We can now follow the WIN "funnel" along its entire course, from assessments through completions (Chart 10).

CHART 10. THERE'S MANY A SLIP . . . IN THE WIN FUNNEL

OF 2,664,000 PERSONS ASSESSED THROUGH FISCAL 1971 . . .

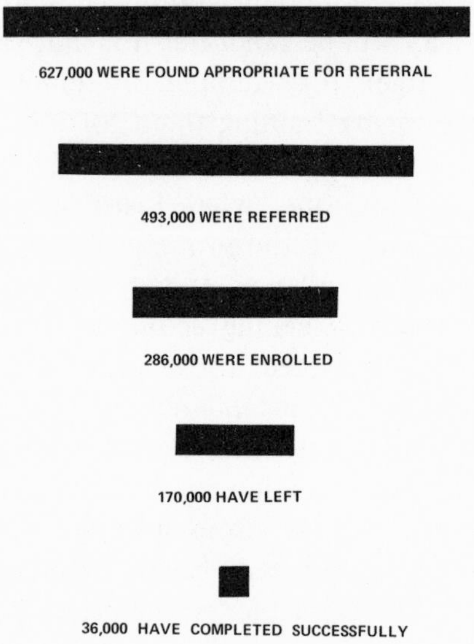

627,000 WERE FOUND APPROPRIATE FOR REFERRAL

493,000 WERE REFERRED

286,000 WERE ENROLLED

170,000 HAVE LEFT

36,000 HAVE COMPLETED SUCCESSFULLY

Source: U.S. Departments of Health, Education, and Welfare, and Labor

COSTS

WIN has been an expensive program, with total federal appropriations of $500 million and outlays of $250 million through fiscal 1971. All federal funds for WIN are appropriated to the Department of Health, Education, and Welfare, with funds for training transferred to the Labor Department. In addition, states share training and child care costs—as they do assistance payments—with the proportion varying by component.

100

Although expenditures have grown steadily, reflecting expansion of program activities, WIN is unique among manpower programs because more money has been appropriated than spent. Many states have been unwilling or unable to raise the required matching funds and have thus limited their overall expenditures. Each state dollar (in cash or in kind) for training was matched by four federal dollars. The federal government paid 85 percent of child care costs until 1970, but then cut their contribution to 75 percent.

Because states were hard pressed financially and less than enthusiastic about WIN, state matching funds were scarce. But in December 1971 an amendment was passed which provided nine federal dollars for each state dollar, for both training and child care.

Widely divergent expenditure patterns between states in large part reflect enrollee characteristics and program components. In California, which has an UF component and where in fiscal 1971 women comprised about one enrollee in ten, child care accounted for only 8 percent of the WIN budget, compared with 43 percent in Georgia, where virtually all enrollees were women, because there is no UF program. Similarly, the educational attainment and previous work experience of enrollees determine the necessity for large basic education, orientation, and work experience components.

Training allowances, child care expenditures, and program administration consume a large proportion of the budget, leaving relatively few funds for actual training. In the four states sampled, the proportion actually spent for training comprised only 31 percent in Georgia, but 61 percent in California (Table 16).

Because costs per man-month varied from about $80 to about $130, total costs per enrollee vary according to duration in the program. Successful completions spend about forty weeks in WIN including follow-up, with the duration a

Table 16. Federal costs for WIN in four states, fiscal year 1971

Component	California	Georgia	Wisconsin	New York
Total (in thousands)	$16,600	$1,700	$3,200	$17,300
(in percent)	100%	100%	100%	100%
Program administration	17	8	8	14
Training	61	31	46	56
Orientation	6	2	8	9
Education	11	2	8	19
On-the-job training	3	1	1	*
Institutional training	21	3	11	12
Work experience	*	*	3	3
Supportive services, other	20	22	15	25
Training and relocation allowances	14	16	21	12
Child care	8	44	25	18
Cost per man-year	$ 950	$1,250	$1,575	$ 1,235

*Less than 0.5 percent.
SOURCE: U.S. Departments of Health, Education, and Welfare, and Labor.

little shorter for men and a little longer for women. Thus, each successful placement, taking about nine months at $80 to $130 per month, incurs costs from $700 to $1,200.

Unfortunately, however, only about one enrollee in five is actually placed successfully. Therefore, accurate cost calculations must adjust for this low completion rate. The GAO derived an estimate of almost $3,600 per successful terminee, while others have estimated total costs at twice that figure. The Labor Department has estimated overall costs per successful placement at around $5,000.[14]

AN ASSESSMENT

The assessment of a program depends very much on the measuring rod used. As noted above, numerous goals have been espoused for WIN and they lead to widely divergent appraisals of the effort. Although the official rhetoric emanating from two administrations and Congress indicated that the primary aim of WIN was to stem the welfare tide, the simple arithmetic of welfare demonstrates WIN's necessary futility to accomplish this goal. Between mid-1969, when WIN was supposed to be implemented in all states, and mid-1971, AFDC grew by one million cases. Cumulative enrollments in WIN through September 1971 totaled 317,000 but not even all of the 43,000 enrollees who successfully completed the WIN course of training left welfare. Thus, Congress' charge to Labor and HEW to use WIN to stem the welfare tide remained exhortation supplemented by little actual accomplishment.

Failure to achieve the unreasonable should not obscure WIN's success at more modest goals. One such is the reduction of welfare dependence among enrollees. On a national level, some 40,000 of 200,000 terminees through September 1971 were found to have left welfare after completing WIN. Even this rather meager level should be discounted because the GAO found that "the Department of Labor's presumption that all reductions and eliminations of AFDC payments following a recipient's participation in WIN are related to the operation of the program . . . is not always realistic."[15]

A more detailed study for the state of Utah yields little more comforting results. Of all terminees from WIN since its inception in fall 1968, only three in ten were still on welfare by October 1970. But this rate varied little with success in WIN. That the proportion among successful WIN terminees differed little from dropouts raises doubts about the net effect of WIN. The difference between the groups suggests that WIN only slightly increases chances of escaping welfare.

Still another criterion is whether WIN has enhanced earnings potential. Most of those who persevere to complete WIN training do reap higher earnings. Women's gains are more substantial than men's. However, even among those placed not all registered gains between their last full-time job and their placement after WIN. Indeed, almost two men in five and one woman in eight gained no increase or might have suffered a loss in earnings. But more than one man in three gained over fifty cents an hour as did three women in five (Table 17).

Table 17. Hourly wage gains of WIN graduates

Hourly gain	Males	Females
Total	100%	100% '
$1.51 or more	9	19
$1.01–$1.50	9	12
$.51–$1.00	18	28
$.26–$.50	13	16
$.01–.25	13	12
No gain, or loss	39	13

SOURCE: Analytic Systems, Inc., *Analysis of WIN Program Termination Data, Fiscal Year 1970.*

Although some of these increases may be substantial, many persons still make too little to escape welfare. Median hourly earnings for females was below $2.00. Three men in ten and nearly three women in five make under $2.00 per hour. Only one man in five and one woman in twenty makes more than $3.00 per hour.

Another critical indicator of the adequacy of these jobs is the number of hours worked weekly. Full-time work was the rule among the WIN placements studied in fiscal 1970, with nine of every ten working 40 or more hours.

The WIN program in general, and earnings levels specifically, can be evaluated by their adequacy in reducing families' assistance payments, even if not completely eliminating them. Although WIN earnings seldom allow graduates to escape AFDC, they are more often sufficient to permit reductions in assistance payments. According to Labor Department data, participation in WIN led to a reduction in assistance for 68,000 families of 200,000 terminees through September 1971. The Labor Department estimated that the level of hourly earnings by former WIN enrollees was adequate to terminate their welfare payments in five states and to halve their welfare payments in thirty-seven states, assuming they continued to work full time. In another two states the welfare payments would have stopped completely if hourly earnings were raised by 50 cents.[8] These computations, however, may overstate the adequacy of WIN earnings because they take account of the "$30 plus 1/3" earnings incentive, but neglect work expenses. After post-WIN earnings are corrected for only moderate work expenses of about $60 per month, the average earnings are inadequate to remove a family from welfare in all states or to halve payments in half the states.

An assessment of WIN is vitally dependent on the criterion specified. In reducing the growth of welfare or moving enrollees off welfare, WIN rates low marks. In raising earnings and reducing welfare payments for "successful" graduates, WIN has performed better. Whether the total effort justified the $250 million in federal outlays for the program during its first three years remains a matter of conjecture.

CONTINUING ISSUES

A Separate Program?

A separate program for welfare recipients made sense in the opening days of the Great Society antipoverty efforts, when there was little experience in serving the disadvantaged and whatever manpower programs were then in existence tended to serve a more selected clientele. But the Labor Department's numerous manpower programs have increasingly sought out and served the disadvantaged. Indeed, WIN transfers some enrollees to other programs and many more welfare recipients enroll directly. It is doubtful whether WIN's variance from other programs in incentives for participation and sanctions for nonattendance serve any useful purpose. There is no convincing evidence that most AFDC recipients face substantially different problems than other manpower clientele, or that they need a separate program simply because of their dependence, which is frequently temporary.

The proliferation of manpower programs for clients who experience difficulties in competing for jobs has served many poor people, but frequently at inordinate costs. Manpower policy-shapers have recognized the need for the consolidation of the diverse categorical efforts. The pending bills before Congress exclude WIN from most designs to consolidate programs for the disadvantaged, not because WIN is unique but because the program is under the jurisdiction of the Ways and Means Committee in the House and the Finance Committee in the Senate. The power of these two committees should not be underestimated. It is not too much to hope, however, that the members of these committees might cede jurisdictional claims over their "own" manpower program in order to improve its efficiency and to better serve the clients.

Child Care

The lack of child care has been a favorite whipping boy for federal officials trying to justify the gap between their promises and WIN's performance. But just as obvious as the necessity of child care for female family heads to enter training or employment is the likelihood that an adequate supply will not be soon forthcoming. Hence, attempts to pin WIN's failures on child care are not likely to be proved wrong. More careful reflection, however, will reveal that success rates for men—who are rarely hampered by the lack of child care—are not substantially more favorable than for women. Thus, the fixation on child care as WIN's major shackle may too frequently serve as an alibi for poor performance.

More Experimentation Needed

Mandatory for states only after July 1969, WIN barely had time to be launched before President Nixon announced his Family Assistance Plan to revamp the welfare system, including a much expanded "workfare" program akin to WIN. During most of WIN's history, the Departments of HEW and Labor have been trying to straddle the fence between WIN and more ambitious efforts under some guaranteed income programs. This has produced the curious spectacle of officials alternately claiming that new training programs for AFDC recipients should be vastly expanded in line with the pending legislation and that WIN was a failure requiring a major overhaul.

A central lesson of the sequence of CWT, WET, and WIN is that a few operational changes, regardless of the rhetoric, can work few miracles. Expansion of a program that has experienced serious difficulties will only multiply the errors. With so massive and far-reaching a program waiting in the wings, there is a pressing need for careful demonstration projects of the principles of welfare reform. The experience of WIN does not justify the promise that an expanded program will enable many welfare recipients to become self-supporting.

NOTES

1. Sar A. Levitan, *Antipoverty Work and Training Efforts: Goals and Reality* (2nd edition; Ann Arbor, Michigan: The Institute of Labor and Industrial Relations, 1968), p. 88.

2. U.S. Department of Labor, Manpower Administration, *Work Incentive Program Handbook*, issued July 1968, Section 101. The Department of Health, Education, and Welfare, through its Social and Rehabilitation Service, issued *Guidelines . . . Work Incentive Program* in July 1969.

3. Frederick B. Arner, *The Work Incentive (WIN) Program: Establishment and Early Implementation*, Library of Congress, Congressional Research Service, June 1969, pp. 70–71.

4. U.S. Department of Labor, *WIN for a Change* (Washington: Government Printing Office, 1971), p. 1, emphasis added.

5. Comptroller General of the United States, *Report of the Congress on Problems in Accomplishing Objectives of the Work Incentive Program (WIN)*, September 1971, p. 30.

6. Edward M. Opton, Jr., *Factors Associated with Employment among Welfare Mothers* (Berkeley, Calif.: The Wright Institute, 1971), prepared under Labor Department Contract No. 51–05–69–04.

7. Andrew K. Solarz, "Effects of the Earnings Exemption Provision on AFDC Recipients," *Welfare in Review* (January–February 1971): 18–20.

8. U.S. Congress, House Committee on Ways and Means, *Hearings on Social Security and Welfare Proposals*, 91st Cong., 1st Sess. (Washington: Government Printing Office, 1970), Part 2, p. 367.

9. U.S. Congress, House Committee on Appropriations, *Hearings on Departments of Labor and Health, Education, and Welfare Appropriations for 1971*, 91st Cong., 2d Sess. (Washington: Government Printing Office, 1970), Part 4, p. 236.

10. U.S. Congress, House Committee on Appropriations, *Hearings on Departments of Labor and Health, Education, and Welfare Appropriations for 1972*, 92d Cong., 1st Sess. (Washington: Government Printing Office, 1971), Part 4, p. 211.

11. U.S. Congress, House Committee on Appropriations, *Hearings on Departments of Labor and Health, Education, and Welfare Appropriations for 1972*, 92d Cong. 1st Sess. (Washington: Government Printing Office, 1971), Part 4, pp. 204–5.

12. Comptroller General of the United States, *Problems in Accomplishing Objectives of the Work Incentive Program (WIN)*, September 1971, pp. 32–35.

13. Olympus Research Corp., *The Total Impact of Manpower Programs: A Four-City Case Study* (Washington: The Corporation, 1971), p. N–25.

14. Testimony of Manpower Administrator Paul J. Fasser, Jr., in U.S. Congress, House Committee on Appropriations, *Hearings on Departments of Labor and Health, Education and Welfare Appropriations*

for 1972 (Washington: Government Printing Office, 1971), Part 4, p. 191.

15. Comptroller General of the United States, *Problems in Accomplishing Objectives of the Work Incentive Program (WIN)*, September 1971, p. 19.

5

Options in Welfare Policy

THE WORK ETHIC

The weakness of the welfare system is now widely recognized. And since this has been acknowledged, the need for a fundamental reform has also been accepted equally by friends and antagonists of the welfare state. Nonetheless, agreement on a politically acceptable alternative has proved elusive. The lack of consensus reflects the difficulty of marshaling pressure for any new system, even though the present network of help is known to be bankrupt.

The basis for so sweeping an indictment of the welfare system arises in part from the inequities of the benefit levels, the rules of eligibility, the adequacy of the grant, and the total income that those on welfare command. But the more immediate cause for concern is the persistent growth of the AFDC program. As we have seen, it grew by 4.4 million people between 1960 and 1969; and in the first eighteen months of the present decade an additional 2.7 million became dependent upon the program. The cost more than tripled during the 1960s, and in 1970 the price tag increased by an additional 41 percent. The cost of the program, and the fiscal crisis that it is presumed to have created in cities and states, is no doubt the most urgent aspect of what has come to be known as the "welfare crisis."

Commenting on these trends in 1971, the House Ways and Means Committee concluded that "attempts to patch up the present system or to close its loopholes simply will not work and would lead to nothing but disillusionment and recrimination."[1] Nearly two years earlier President Nixon had proposed sweeping reform because "the present welfare system has to be judged a colossal failure . . . failing to meet the elementary human, social, and financial needs of the poor. It breaks up homes. If often penalizes work. It robs recipients of dignity. And it grows."[2] But the efforts of two succeeding Congresses have not been able to translate this broad commitment into specific policies that help reduce the size and cost of the welfare caseload. Despite the priority placed on welfare reform by both the President and the Congress, difficulties arise because there is an ambivalence about objectives and because there are contradictions in the reform strategy pursued.

The guiding principle of welfare reform is the work ethic requiring employable welfare recipients to earn income through work rather than to rely upon welfare alone. The welfare reformers assume that jobs can be generated for all those who are able to work and that training can be provided for all those who can be made employable. This assumption suggests that assistance be given to individuals who work but earn less than those on welfare. Public assistance is then expected to serve as a final net for those who cannot work, providing an "adequate" floor of income to all the poor, regardless of residence or source of income. These principles of work, training, adequate benefits, and equitable treatment form the mold from which specific legislative programs can be cast.

The Social Security Act of 1935 enabled mothers to remain outside the labor force if they chose benefits rather than employment and to raise their children in their own homes. Spurred by the increasing numbers of mothers who have entered the work force in the past three decades, the thrust of the reforms in the past decade has been to induce more welfare mothers to seek work. Congress has assisted some needy families to achieve this goal. In the words of the welfare reform bill approved by the House in 1971, the objective is to provide: "members of needy families with children the manpower services, training, employment, child care, family planning, and related services which are necessary to train them, prepare them for employment, and otherwise assist them in securing and retaining regular employment and having the opportunity for advancement in employment, to the end that such families will be restored to self-supporting independent and useful roles in their communities."

These work-related objectives for the AFDC program are no new departure. They have been emerging in Congress for more than a decade. In 1956 three broadly defined objectives of welfare legislation were economic independence, self-help, and the strengthening of family life. The federal administrators of the program tended to stress the latter two goals more than the first. But the priorities soon shifted. The 1961 Social Security Amendments qualified unemployed parents to receive federal public assistance and made untenable the presumption that all welfare recipients were unemployed. This legislation stimulated the search for means to help employable parents work their way off the relief rolls.

By 1967 the House Ways and Means Committee announced its intention of setting "a new direction for AFDC legislation" by recommending "a series of amendments to carry out its firm intent of reducing the AFDC rolls by restoring more families to employment and self-reliance."[3] Four years later the House reaffirmed its commitment to establish a new course for welfare policy, although the Senate balked at the added costs required by this approach. The new policy of encouraging those in receipt of cash benefits to secure work calls for new principles to guide the distribution of benefits. It may be useful to sketch out these principles, to explain their underlying rationale, and to examine some of the problems they present.

PRINCIPLES UNDERLYING WORK INCENTIVE POLICIES

Assuming that welfare recipients should be induced to work, one approach is to provide them with economic incentives to enter the labor force without necessarily denying them public assistance. Essentially the incentive approach integrates employment income into the benefit structure, and it provides that the reduction in benefits should be less than any increase in employment earnings until the family reaches a predetermined level of income. The income of families with working adults would exceed that of families whose incomes depended solely on benefits, and for this reason the incentive approach might also be regarded as an income strategy. The crucial flaw of the welfare system until 1967 was that it often reduced welfare benefits dollar for dollar against increased earnings after allowances had been made for work-connected expenses. Since this system left the family at work no better off economically, it created no incentive for employment.

Proponents of the incentive approach anticipate that the additional income provided to public assistance recipients will not only raise their incomes in the short run but will encourage them toward long-range economic independence as their income from work continues to rise. It is hoped that welfare recipients whose earnings are subjected to low

113

marginal tax rates will be encouraged to work. The task then is to design a system under which extra earnings are not offset by substantial reductions in welfare payments and other benefits.

Income strategies designed to serve as incentives to work have been widely referred to as negative income taxation. They all share the following characteristics: they maintain an income floor for all persons whose resources fall below the established level; recipients keep some proportion of any additional dollars earned; and the value of the income guarantee is reduced as earnings increase up to a break-even point at which benefits cease.

The 1967 Social Security Amendments embraced the negative income tax principle, though on a modest scale, as one means of "restoring more families to employment and self-reliance." The act required state and local welfare departments to disregard for the purpose of benefit eligibility the first $30 in monthly earnings and one-third of all earnings above this amount. These provisions are known as the "$30 and 1/3 rule." In addition, actual work-related expenses are also disregarded from earnings.

The aim of the 1967 negative income tax was to create a positive incentive for benefit recipients to seek work; it was much less concerned with providing income assurance for all those who fell below some minimally defined level of acceptability. States continued to set their own floor of protection. The legislation focused on earning retention, not on a guaranteed level of income, although it did require states to revise their standards of need to take account of changes in the cost of living.

Once the concept had been accepted in principle, the debate turned to the parameters necessary to make the negative income tax effective. The income floor had to be low enough, as a proportion of net average earnings, and the tax rate had to be sufficiently attractive so that in combination they would encourage work. No one knew exactly what the most effective combinations of guarantee and marginal tax rates were to achieve this aim, but this was regarded as a technical problem to be solved by social experiments that would test the effects of various combinations.

Economists differed on this important technical question. James Tobin of Yale University, considered a "liberal" economist, advocated a low guarantee and a low marginal tax rate, allowing welfare recipients to retain a higher proportion of their earnings. He favored a guaranteed annual income of only $400 per individual, but would have allowed the family to retain two-thirds of its earnings. Thus a family of four with an earned income of $3,000 would lose $1,000 of its guaranteed income of $1,600, receiving a $600 subsidy and a total income of $3,600. The President's Commission on Income Maintenance Programs favored a higher floor: $750 per adult and $450 per child, with a provision that payments be reduced by 50 percent for each dollar of income earned.

The income strategy was directed at providing an incentive to work. But the will to work on its own was clearly insufficient if it was not reinforced by the availability of jobs and training facilities that could provide opportunities to acquire necessary skills. A complementary approach, therefore, focusing on broadening opportunities for work, seemed equally essential. Such an approach could move in two directions—toward job assurance and skill acquisition.

One popular proposal to guarantee employment requires the government to assume responsibility as the "employer of last resort," standing ready to employ all persons who are unable to secure regular work in the private market. This work-guarantee principle could be pursued in the private sector as well by having the government reimburse employers for any extra costs involved in hiring, training, and retaining relief recipients. Under this arrangement the private employer would pay a socially acceptable minimum, and the government would pay the employer the difference between the wages paid and the actual worth of the workers. But an employment guarantee raises questions about its impact upon discipline in the marketplace. Would recalcitrant workers be paid even if they shirked work or performed poorly?

In addition to providing guaranteed work through public employment or wage supplements, the government could help individuals acquire, through training and supportive social services, the skills necessary to secure jobs. Confident that jobs are available, public policy can emphasize manpower training and facilitate access to jobs by expanding transportation possibilities and encouraging relocation.

Clearly, some combination of guaranteed employment, together with manpower training and incentives, could be pursued. But it would also be possible to create the form of a training program without its substance by having the training perform a cash transfer function. Training grants that provide a cash subsidy large enough to sustain individuals can also substitute for welfare payments, at least for the duration of the training. Some training programs, such as the Neighborhood Youth Corps programs, appear essentially to offer cash transfers under the guise of training. Here the distinctions between employment, training, and cash grants are blurred.

Public policy in the 1960s accepted all three principles—payment of cash incentives, job creation, and training and work-related services—but assigned a different priority to each. Although public funds have been used to experiment on a modest scale with relocation subsidies to families and to employers, the idea of guaranteed jobs has not received wide acceptance. It was the work training and supportive services, combined with the "$30 and 1/3" incentive, that gained center stage in the 1967 Amendments to the Social Security Act. These amendments were designed to effect a decline in caseloads both by increasing skills through job training and services and by broadening work incentives.

Acceptance of the 1967 amendments was not without controversy. Granted the desirability of providing welfare recipients with incentives to work, the debate centered on whether these provisions should be voluntary or compulsory. John Gardner, then Secretary of Health, Education, and Welfare, took the position that work training should be mandatory for the states and voluntary for individuals. But his views were rejected by the majority of the members of the House Ways and Means Committee, who insisted that the work training program be compulsory. The debate ended in a compromise, reflected in the provisions of the work incentive program, and limited the AFDC cases to which compulsory employment or training applied. The issue of coercion or voluntary participation has remained unsettled and controversial in and out of Congress. Work requirements for selected groups in 1967 were accepted in principle and frustrated in practice. The law also attempted to provide an economic incentive for states to implement the principles of training and work by freezing the federally supported caseload at the 1968 level. The freeze was never implemented and the AFDC rolls continued to mount. States already in a financial bind prevailed upon Congress to continue paying the federal share of public assistance.

POLICY ALTERNATIVES

The efforts to transform public assistance into a work-oriented system represent only one aspect of the debate about reducing poverty at a minimum cost to the taxpayers.

117

A pervasive confusion between the aims of reducing poverty and reforming welfare has seemed unavoidable, since the income strategies proposed to implement both of these aims appear to be similar. However, a strategy directed primarily at reducing poverty rather than at encouraging work suggests alternative principles of intervention.

The most widely debated alternative is to pay families with children a regular allowance to supplement their own income and to meet some portion of the costs of child-rearing. This proposal recognizes that the wage system distributes income inadequately because wages are based on productivity or on tradition rather than on family need. The principle of equal pay for equal work is desirable as a protection against discrimination based on color or sex, but it ignores the differing needs of families and tends to deprive children in large families of their basic necessities. The underlying justification for family allowances is that the child's well-being should concern society at large. But if these allowances were concentrated on those with the lowest incomes, they could serve as a transfer program for the poor and as a subsidy for the working poor with large families. Although children's allowances are used widely in western industrial countries, this approach has not received active legislative consideration in the United States, partly because it does not serve as a direct and obvious strategy for encouraging participation in the labor force and partly because of apprehensions that it might raise birth rates.

Yet another approach is to utilize the tax structure to provide income to the poor. Currently geared for the collection of taxes alone, the tax reporting machinery could be adapted to distribute grants to cover income deficits—a negative income tax. Such an income support scheme, like a family allowance, could be related to the number of dependents and thus act as an income supplement to the working poor. A related proposal is to refund social security taxes paid by low-income workers.

A third approach is through guaranteed income maintenance. Such schemes seek to reduce poverty through a reformed, comprehensive, national, and probably greatly expanded, welfare system. This approach explicitly rejects the presumption embodied in the Social Security Act of 1935 that public assistance would be a residual program, eventually giving way to the contributory insurance system to perform the transfer functions. The advocates of a national, comprehensive welfare system would stand the 1935 act "on its head" by making welfare the basic income support program rather than such a residual measure for the relief of distress.

WELFARE REFORM: THE CONFLICT BETWEEN POVERTY REDUCTION AND WORK INCENTIVES

It is useful to distinguish the strategies to reduce poverty from the efforts to reform the welfare system by emphasizing "rehabilitation." Although the means overlap, and problems of reconciling costs, incentives, and efficiency are similar, the purposes diverge.

Welfare reform has an internal logic of its own, but the combined aims of reducing rolls, encouraging work, and reducing poverty also suggest anomalies. For example, reform maintains a simultaneous commitment to expanded coverage and decreased costs, and there are inherent conflicts between adequate benefits and work incentives. These problems cannot be resolved, but they can be mitigated by administrative reforms.

The President's Commission on Income Maintenance Programs (the Heineman Commission), appointed by President Johnson in 1968 to study the income needs of the poor, advocated poverty reduction through both a tested income guarantee and the promotion of incentives for work. The Commission recommended a universal income supplement program $2,400 at a marginal tax of 50 percent, federally financed and administered to cover all the poor. The proposal would, in 1970, have added about $6 billion net income for 10 million families. Of this, $5 billion would have gone to the poor, making it a relatively efficient program. By this single effort, half of the income needs of the poor would have been met.

Other proposals would have raised the income floor higher. However, as the minimum guarantee is raised, inefficiencies begin to emerge. Based on a 1970 income distribution, only 36 percent of the aggregate cost of a program guaranteeing an annual income of $3,600 to a family of four and a 50 percent tax on earnings would have gone to the poor. Moreover, costs are also bound to increase sharply as the minimum guarantee level is raised without changing the tax rate or as the tax rate is lowered for a given guarantee level. The cost of raising the minimum benefit therefore grows progressively higher simply because there are more families with earnings in each higher interval. In addition, there is an erosion of the tax base as those below the break-even point are exempted from positive taxes. In 1970 a basic annual allowance of $2,400 for a family of four would have cost $8 billion; at $3,000 costs would have been raised to $14 billion; at $3,600 to $22 billion; and at the $6,500 level recommended by the National Welfare Rights Organization, costs would have exceeded $66 billion.[4]

The subtle relationship between negative and positive tax rates requires elaboration. If the principle of preserving work incentives is not to be compromised, then a reform of the positive tax system must accompany the introduction of negative taxes. When personal income and social security taxes are imposed on families receiving benefits below the break-even point, they are unavoidably subjected to high marginal tax rates. For a family of four, positive taxes on income above $3,650 are at least 14 percent, and social security taxes take out another 5.2 percent up to an income level of $7,800. Thus, in addition to a high tax on benefits, welfare recipients would also be subject to an additional 19.2 percent in other federal taxes. The effective tax rate of those poor aspiring to economic independence would thus be raised to 69.2 percent, assuming a 50 percent tax on income above disregarded earnings in addition to normal tax rates. If such excessive tax rates are to be avoided, there must be an increase in taxes on higher incomes to cover these costs; but in addition the entire tax system must also become sharply more progressive, since large numbers of wage earners will also escape payment of taxes. An adequate guaranteed level and effective incentives are not only costly but require a public commitment to progressive taxation and income redistribution toward the lower half of the wage structure. It seems doubtful that so fundamental a reform will be accepted as the price of reducing poverty and preserving work incentives.

This problem can be reduced, but not avoided, by restricting coverage to families with children and by accepting higher marginal tax rates. This can be illustrated by consideration of the family program passed by the House in 1971 (H.R. 1). This program calls for a $2,400 allowance for a family of four persons and a 66.7 percent tax rate on earnings above $720. The staff of the Committee estimated that increasing benefits by $100 and "keeping other parts of the benefit structure the same, raises the breakeven point by $150, increases the cost by over $500 million per year and the number of eligible families by 300 thousand."[5]

Income supplements, efficiency, and low expenditure outlays can be achieved only at a low level of payments. The problem is somewhat attenuated by a decrease in the proportion of earned income retained or the level of the income disregards, since these changes lower the break-even point and reduce the number of eligible recipients. But such an approach also diminishes the work incentive features of the negative income tax. There is a persistent and unresolvable conflict, inherent in the structure of the scheme, between the three principles of encouraging work incentives through lower tax rates, reducing poverty by assuring adequate minimum levels of subsistence, and maintaining "reasonable" costs. Trade-offs among these principles weaken one at the cost of another, but cost consciousness undermines both strategies, producing a diffuse sense of malaise and dissatisfaction.

While the overall orientation and rhetoric of welfare reform has been to strengthen the commitment to work, developments in other programs to alleviate poverty have conflicted with this goal. The most serious conflict has been between the expansion of in-kind programs to meet the basic necessities of food, shelter, and medical care and the low incentives offered to induce welfare recipients to work. In-kind benefits have undermined work efforts by making relief more attractive. The presumed cash incentives offered by the Nixon administration, and seriously considered by Congress, have in fact offered little pecuniary incentive to encourage relief recipients to work.

Although H.R. 1 proposed a 67 percent tax rate on annual earnings above $720, the real rate was higher. Because social security and income taxes rise with earnings, net cash income rises slowly between $2,000 and $6,000. When the value of possible in-kind benefits such as Medicaid and public housing is included, the incentives will be even less attractive (Table 18).

The high tax rate threatened the entire rationale of welfare reform, namely, that people should always be better off if they worked than if they were on welfare. As a result, the

Table 18. Benefits potentially available to a four-person female-headed
family in Chicago, under H.R. 1

Earn-ings[a]	Federal benefit	State supple-ment	Taxes		TOTAL, net cash income	Medic-aid[b]	Hous-ing[c]
			Income	Social security			
None[d]	$2,400	$1,392	—	—	$3,792	$910	$1,416
$2,000	1,546	1,392	—	$104	4,834	684	1,089
3,000	879	1,392	—	156	5,115	570	908
4,000	213	1,392	—	208	5,397	456	728
5,000	—	938	$164	260	5,514	342	547
6,000	—	271	349	312	5,610	228	367
7,000	—	—	545	364	6,091	114	186
8,000	—	—	723	416	6,861	—	6
9,000	—	—	908	468	7,624	—	—

[a]According to the Bureau of Labor Statistics, fringe benefits may add signifi-cantly to the value of work, from $350 at $3,000 annual earnings to $3,600 at $9,000.

[b]According to HEW, $910 is the average Medicaid payment on behalf of all families in Illinois. Individual families may receive higher or lower value depend-ing upon medical needs. H.R. 1 provides a "spend-down" for Medicaid coverage, so that benefits will decline as income increases. However, HEW has not yet calculated the variation in benefits because it depends on "complex actuarial factors which vary from family to family." For present purposes, we have assumed a straight-line "spend-down," which creates less work disincentive than other methods.

[c]Available to 18 percent of AFDC recipients in Chicago.

[d]Assumes no one in family is required to register for work or training.

SOURCE: U.S. Department of Health, Education, and Welfare.

Senate Finance Committee raised doubts about the adminis-tration's commitment to an effective incentive program.

The dilemma faced in attempts to reform welfare is clear. If the in-kind programs and mandatory state cash supple-ments were removed and benefits maintained at a low level, then incentives to work would be increased—but only at the cost of the well-being of most recipients. Adequate benefits to relieve poverty conflict with a coherent incentive system to encourage work.

The erosion of work incentives through the compounding of tax rates is of serious concern to the advocates of an adequate negative income tax. Their goal can be achieved only at a cost. Inherent in any such plan is a low tax on earnings above a guaranteed income. The higher level of disregards qualifies ever more people to retain a portion of their assistance and requires that cash assistance be retained at seemingly unacceptable levels. According to some plans, public assistance would not be stopped until the total income of recipients reached $6,000 or more. Such plans would qualify one-fourth of all American families to benefit from the negative tax plan. The most ardent welfare reformers will have to concede that the taxpayer must also receive some consideration from those who want to improve the lot of the poor.

All the good will and exhortation of welfare reformers have failed to offer a viable solution to the welfare dilemma. There is no way to provide generous public assistance that will raise all families above the poverty threshold as long as our wage structure fails to provide adequate earnings to those who work. Nearly one of every seven persons employed in 1970 earned less than $2.00 per hour, an amount which would barely raise a family of four above poverty if earned for full-time work, year round. Of all family heads with work experience in 1970, about 4 percent remained in poverty although they worked full time for most or all of the year. And the incidence of poverty rose rapidly among those who could find work or chose to work less—including 14 percent of those who worked full time for more than half the year or part time for most or all of the year.

Public policy, when confronted with a dilemma for which there is no inherent solution, tends to pursue one aspect of it; then when the limits of this approach become evident, it is repudiated and an alternative approach embraced. Some already argue that welfare has over-responded to political pressure for more adequate benefits and has in some places exceeded the limits of generosity; adherents of this view urge retrenchment of the welfare program by restricting the number of persons who receive benefits and by decreasing cash benefit levels, Medicaid, and food programs. About a dozen states pursued such a course during 1971. The axiom that political decisionmakers cannot feasibly pursue policies that make individuals worse off apparently does not hold for welfare recipients who have little political clout.

ISSUES IN CURRENT WELFARE REFORM PROPOSALS

National administration, low benefits, wider coverage, work and training requirements, access to supportive services, and earnings retention comprise the main elements of the welfare reform design that Congress has been groping toward since the 1962 Social Security Amendments. The claim that this movement represents a radical departure from established practice misrepresents the continuities with the past. The reforms pending are better understood as an attempt to work out the inherent problems encountered by previous efforts.

President Nixon's Family Assistance Act was originally introduced on October 3, 1969. Though the House approved it with relatively minor changes in April 1970, the Senate Finance Committee balked. Liberals felt that the level of payments was inadequate, while conservatives objected to any guaranteed income, no matter what banner it was sold under. A compromise might have been reached on the level of benefits, but the Senate Finance Committee could not agree on a satisfactory work incentive design, and the Senate failed to act on President Nixon's welfare reform during the 91st Congress.

The Family Assistance Act was reintroduced, in similar form, in the 92nd Congress. The House approved the welfare legislation in June 1971 by an even larger margin, 288 to 131, than in the preceding year. But the Senate Finance Committee remained divided on the proposed reform legislation and failed to report out the bill.

The Senate Finance Committee could not resolve the conflict of welfare reform and poverty reduction consistent with work incentive principles at a reasonable cost. Combined, these issues of incentives, adequacy, and cost created the trilemma of welfare reform. Swayed by Wilbur Mills, chairman of the House Ways and Means Committee, and by strong support from the Nixon administration, the House compromised by approving a very low minimum income guarantee and, to assuage conservatives, adopted the rhetoric of coercive work requirements. No such compromise emerged in the Senate. The controversy centered on four critical issues: coverage; benefit levels and tax rates; reliance on in-kind benefits for basic necessities; and the role of work, training, and supportive services.

Coverage

The welfare reform embodied in the House-approved H.R. 1 would increase the number of welfare recipients from 15 million in 1973 by an additional 11 million persons. Included would be about 2.5 million families in which the head of household worked during the previous year—more than two-fifths of whom worked full time, year round but remained in poverty (Table 19). Only about one-third of the family heads who would qualify for assistance under H.R. 1 would have worked at all during the previous year. The reform legislation would thus not only enlarge the scope of welfare but would redefine its function from being primarily a substitute to a supplement for wages. If the working poor

126

were generally included with the AFDC program, this would also alter the racial composition of the program, as the projected proportion of nonwhite families would decline from 48 to 38 percent.

Table 19. Work experience of families eligible for family payments under H.R. 1

	Total families	Male heads	Female heads
TOTAL	3,815	1,819	1,995
Worked full or part time	2,460	1,546	943
Worked full year			
(50 to 52 weeks)	1,272	932	341
Full time	1,113	857	256
Part time	159	74	85
Worked part year			
(less than 50 weeks)	1,188	568	601
Full time	859	489	371
Part time	329	97	232
Did not work at all	1,355	273	1,052

SOURCE: U.S. Congress, House Committee on Ways and Means, *Report on H.R. 1, Social Security Amendments of 1971*, p. 231.

Why did the House Ways and Means Committee, critical of the size of the welfare population, favor further expansion? The most obvious answer is that effective incentives require broad coverage. Secretary Finch, in response to Senator Byrd's questioning, offered the following explanation of the administration's desire to expand the welfare rolls: "We think that helping the working poor is absolutely indispensable to the whole program. It is the only way we think we can come to grips with work incentives and prevent the low wage worker from dropping into welfare. It induces . . . a man on welfare to want to get a better job."[6]

Yet another reason to include the working poor is to avoid the anomalies of an incentive program limited to those presently on welfare. As it is, those who work while on welfare can acquire higher total incomes (when grants, earnings, and in-kind benefits are added) than those in full-time employment. But reducing the inequities between current welfare recipients and the working poor is costly; as a result, legislative proposals have accepted the principle of inclusion without granting equal treatment. Thus, the working poor have not been automatically entitled to income supplements above the federal guaranteed minimum or to Medicaid, as are current AFDC recipients.

The House Ways and Means Committee refused to rely solely upon the built-in economic work incentives or upon federal and state officials to carry out the intent of the legislation. Instead, the bill required many adult recipients to register for training or employment. The Committee made a determined effort to spell out exemptions from this requirement: the ill; the incapacitated; the elderly; a mother or other relative caring for a child under six (after July 1974 for a child under three); a dependent youth between sixteen and twenty-two if attending school; a person needed in the home to care for an ill member of the household. This attempt to define explicitly who should be required to take training or enter employment reflects congressional irritation with responsible officials who are "soft" on welfare recipients. The employability status of the present and potential AFDC population was thus being altered by definition. However, the bill did not create enough jobs for all employable relief recipients and left doubt about the efficacy of the incentives provided.

Benefit Level and Tax Rate

The Ways and Means proposal in 1971 called for a uniform income guarantee of $1,600 for a family of two persons, $400 for each of the next three family members, $300 for the next two, and $200 for each additional member. Thus, a family of two adults and two children with no other income would receive $2,400 per year. Benefits would not be reduced until annual earnings had exceeded $720, and thereafter would be reduced by two dollars for each additional three dollars earned. For a family of four, cash benefits would cease when earnings reached $4,260. While the supplements or earnings would have boosted the incomes of many working poor, the guaranteed income proposed was not generous by 1971 standards. Ninety percent of welfare recipients—those living in 45 states and the District of Columbia—already received more substantial benefits than the proposed minimum federal guarantee, and the bill did not require these states to supplement federal payments to maintain existing benefit levels. If such states were to decide to supplement the federal benefit and to maintain their present payment levels, including an increase to take account of the loss of the value of the food stamp bonus, then they would also have to let the federal government administer the supplementary payment. States agreeing to these arrangements were assured that their expenditures would not exceed welfare outlays incurred in calendar 1971, and as a bonus they were also assured a net saving for five years equal to the cost of administering the program.

Although H.R. 1 would initially have raised the costs of welfare, it was intended to avoid larger outlays in the future. And the present mounting costs of welfare are persuasive evidence that the trend is likely to continue. Administration spokesmen projected, or hoped, that the rise in costs would taper off and eventually decline, anticipating that the income supplements and work incentives would encourage work and economic independence. The House and the administration hoped that raising the monthly earnings exemption from $30 to $60 (but denying work-connected expenses) and maintaining a 66.7 percent tax rate on all annual earnings above $720 would accomplish the trick. Conventional wisdom holds that marginal tax rates above one-half of earnings seriously discourage any work effort because the individual is then "earning" more for the government than for himself. The Committee, however, decided to restrict the work-incentive provision, partly to reduce costs and partly to avoid another anomaly created by high incentives, that of families with relatively high incomes still qualifying for welfare payments.

Moreover, the proposed increase in the flat income disregard, to $60 per month from the $30 provided in the 1967 legislation, is misleading. The 1967 law provided that all work-related expenses were to be exempt from welfare deductions. The proposed "reforms" included work-connected expenses within the $60 monthly disregard, and by leaving unchanged the marginal tax above the flat disregard, the House-approved law provided few additional work incentives beyond those included in existing legislation. And, indeed, since many welfare departments already interpreted work expenses liberally, in these states the new reforms reduced existing work-incentive provisions. Policy appears to be moving in the direction of weakening the incentive to work while at the same time raising the benefit levels for those at the lowest end of the benefit structure and providing wage supplements to the working poor. Thus low-level adequacy is purchased at the cost of more effective incentives. Still uneasy about the trade off between tax rates and benefit levels, Congress in 1971 placed even more reliance upon administrative requirements for individuals to register for work and to accept training and employment than had seemed necessary in 1967, and did so without raising payments. The stronger the work requirements, the more credible become the charges of coercion. In response, it is claimed that some protections will be provided. For example, individuals will not be required to accept jobs vacated by labor disputes or paying less than 75 percent of the federal minimum wage, and they will not be required to accept jobs when they can take advantage of other *available* training or employment opportunities. Individuals will also be able to refuse a job where no adequate transportation is available or where child care facilities are lacking. But to make the work requirements effective, penalties will be imposed. If an adult refuses training or employment, $800 annually will be subtracted from his family's benefit checks. The Secretary of Labor also has the option of handing over the responsibility for administering the remaining family payments to someone outside the family who is interested in or concerned with the welfare of the family. A failure to accept training or employment might result, therefore, not only in a loss of income but also in control over the remaining family grant.

The weaker the incentive "carrots," and the stronger the need for compulsory "sticks," the more serious becomes the charge that work requirements will expand the supply of low-cost labor, thus lowering wage levels. As incentives on earnings are abandoned to contain costs, the ideals of welfare reform are replaced by coercive measures that compel work and replace welfare benefits with earnings rather than supplementary earnings.

Benefits In-Kind

The initial debate on FAP (Family Assistance Program) by the Senate Finance Committee in the summer of 1970 centered on the disincentive effects of in-kind programs. Higher earnings not only disqualified families from receiving cash grants but also eroded their entitlement to valuable in-kind benefits. When the Senate Finance Committee brought to light the problems associated with in-kind benefits, this seriously undermined the validity of the assumption that families would be better off working than on welfare, and it threatened the credibility of the FAP program.

The April 1970 hearings focused on the work disincentive effects presented by the "notch" problem. This problem arises when the benefit from a cash or in-kind program is reduced abruptly when earnings reach some specified point. Such a "notch" acts as an explicit work disincentive, since an increase in earnings produces a greater drop in income. For example, a $100 rise in income may disqualify a family from Medicaid—which may be worth several hundred dollars, or far more than the increase in earnings.

The Administration tried to avoid the notch problem by changing eligibility requirements to Medicaid, food stamps, and public housing rather than by modifying the proposed cash provisions. Essentially, the proposed adjustments would involve a tapering off in the value of in-kind benefits so that they would gradually reduce the value of the benefits as earnings were increased. But elimination of anomalies which create a steady decline in total income still do not encourage families to opt for work rather than public assistance. Russell B. Long, chairman of the Senate Finance Committee, advocated during the course of his Committee's hearings on FAP that employable relief recipients should be paid solely for work performed. He argued with Secretary Richardson: "It seems to me that fundamental to your problem here is the fact that you are paying $238 a month—and this is leaving out public housing—to an able-bodied female for doing zero. . . . So from that point forward your incentives all break down . . . the point we have been making here since the day you appeared before this committee on this matter, has been that the incentive is so inadequate that it achieves little or nothing."

HEW Secretary Elliot Richardson, speaking for the administration, conceded that it was essential to smooth the notch problems; but given the limited resources for welfare, he agreed there was little left to provide strong incentives. The Secretary made the choice explicit by explaining that "The Committee will have to decide whether it placed the higher premium on the elimination of any cutoff point at which an individual's income drops, in order to have a steeper incentive line before that, or, to do what we have recommended, which is to flatten the incentive line in order to eliminate the notches." The Secretary estimated that it would cost an additional $6–$7 billion to drop the tax rate on earned income from 50 to 30 percent and that these greater incentives would add 3,200,000 families to the program.[7]

In its 1971 welfare reform bill, the House Ways and Means Committee determined to eliminate or restrict in-kind benefits. H.R. 1 explicitly excluded recipients of family welfare payments from any food program but substituted cash for food benefits, raising the level of the grant from $1,600 to $2,400.

Medical care was more complicated. Individuals in receipt of cash benefits were also automatically entitled to Medicaid. The Committee was concerned not only about the disincentive effect of a termination of this benefit but was also reluctant to have means-tested benefits extended to higher income groups.

The Committee tried to correct both these difficulties by making the standards of eligibility for Medicaid and welfare more consistent. Families with incomes above the cut-off line for Medicaid who were receiving cash assistance could continue to receive Medicaid coverage only after they had incurred medical expenses equal to or larger than the difference between their total income and the Medicaid standard of eligibility. Thus, states would be required to provide medical assistance to all individuals, whether recipients of cash assistance or not, whose incomes (after deducting medical expenses) fell below the medical assistance level (133 percent above the welfare level plus a $720 earned income disregard). While this would avoid situations where an additional dollar of earning could result in a complete loss of protection worth several hundreds of dollars, it would also deny Medicaid to families whose incomes exceeded the eligibility standard, even if they remained on welfare. The Department of Health, Education, and Welfare estimated that these restrictions would yield an annual saving to the federal government of $140 million.

Training, Work, and Supportive Services

As indicated in the previous chapter, training is intended to enhance the employability and earnings potential of recipients, and the monthly $30 cash incentive was designed to make the training pay off immediately. In making training mandatory, the 1971 legislation was reaffirming a provision of the 1967 amendments. But the limited number of training slots available had forced selection of priorities, and many welfare agencies made training optional through lenient enforcement. The new legislation also insisted that when training was not available or appropriate, individuals would be expected to work. This, of course, raised questions about the nature of the jobs that recipients would be obliged to accept. The Department of Labor claimed that it did not contemplate referring recipients to domestic day work jobs. Yet there may be few alternatives available to unskilled and poorly educated recipients if training facilities are limited.

The experience of the WIN program and its antipoverty predecessors has shown that the training of welfare recipients is frequently frustrated because jobs are not available. Welfare recipients normally qualify for low-paying jobs in secondary labor markets, and in loose labor markets jobs are in limited supply; if those not seeking work were forced to do so, the job shortage would become even more acute. To overcome the weaknesses of WIN, the 1971 welfare reform bill proposed to set aside $800 million to provide some 200,000 public service jobs. These jobs, however, would not be intended as permanent. The circumstances of each job-holder would be reviewed every six months to determine whether a more appropriate position could be secured on the regular payroll. This emphasis on transitional jobs must be interpreted in part as a safeguard against the displacement of regular public workers and as prevention against make-work jobs for relief recipients. To assure that the federal government has continued knowledge of job openings, the Labor Department already requires employers who have substantial federal contracts to list their job vacancies with the public employment service. But this requirement will have to be vigorously implemented to be effective.

Training and jobs may also be insufficient, especially where mothers must make arrangements for the care of their children. The welfare reform legislation makes substantial improvements over the earlier WIN provisions for day care. It is hoped that full federal funding of public or private profit and nonprofit agencies to provide child care, and expected revisions of unreasonable licensing requirements will be sufficient to remove some of the child care bottlenecks.

Still many unresolved questions remained. In the attempt to put more welfare recipients to work, the issues raised under WIN still continue to be critical. Are jobs available in the private marketplace? If not, is it worth while to subsidize employment, even beyond the 200,000 jobs to be provided through public service employment? Are the high costs of day care, training, and subsidies justified?

Whether the reform package of training, more liberal work incentives, and increased day care is a wise investment to achieve greater employability of relief recipients is uncertain. Experience with earlier training programs for public assistance recipients does not justify great optimism or rapid expansion of the program. The costs per trainee will be higher and the probable average benefits less because the program will be serving a larger and necessarily more disadvantaged clientele.

The $2.25 billion Public Employment Program, enacted in late 1971, is a modest attempt to provide jobs for public assistance recipients, who filled about one-ninth of the 140,000 slots created. The impact of using public sector jobs to hire a larger concentration of relief recipients is being tested through $50 million in demonstration grants to thirteen areas.

WILL PUBLIC ASSISTANCE REMAIN A MARGINAL PROGRAM?

The welfare reform proposals considered by Congress in 1970 and 1971 have departed very little in principle from earlier legislation, except in providing income supplements to the working poor. The House Ways and Means Committee has remained confident that the basic principles of the 1967 legislation were valid, and it has laid the blame for the lackluster record of the succeeding four years on bungling bureaucracies at the federal, state, and local level. To overcome the fragmented responsibility for training and cash payments that led to administrative muddles, Congress in 1971 moved to centralize authority within the Department of Labor, but postponed action on centralizing the whole cash assistance program.

After consideration of lower marginal tax rates as an incentive to encourage welfare recipients to seek work, the 1971 legislative proposals have retained the marginal tax rate embodied in the 1967 legislation; they have raised the guarantee level proposed in 1970, but only at the cost of commensurate in-kind benefits.

Emphasis on training has continued to be central to the proposed welfare legislation. The expansion of jobs in public employment has been added as a link between training and employment. The earlier social work emphasis on total family needs has been replaced by more specific supportive services, such as child care and family planning.

The conflict between adequate benefits to reduce poverty and the preservation of the incentive system to encourage work has tended to produce an increased reliance on coercion, requiring individuals to accept work and training. But whatever the potential effectiveness of coercion in encouraging economic independence, the tactics may be undermined in loose labor markets. If competition for jobs is intense, newly created public employment jobs cannot be reserved exclusively for welfare recipients when more qualified, unemployed workers are seeking an inadequate number of jobs. A commitment to tight labor markets is essential to the success of a policy that requires public assistance recipients to train for jobs. But tight labor markets are accompanied by inflationary pressures. Economic policy has been unable to master both tight labor markets and stable prices, and public policy may continue to favor dampening inflation at the cost of slack labor markets. The latest attempt to trade off inflation for higher unemployment resulted in both high unemployment and inflation, with the poor as victims of both ills.

A public policy intent on transforming the welfare system into a major instrument for reducing poverty and also for self-liquidating welfare, by converting it into a manpower program, is bound to rely upon coercion and to produce frustrating results. There are no easy solutions to the rising welfare costs, and whatever reforms emerge, welfare will

137

continue to be a persistent issue during the 1970s. A realistic and viable approach is to recognize that there is a growing interdependence between welfare and work and that for ever-increasing numbers the two go together. The challenge is to win political backing for an income-support program that will encourage dependents to work even if they do not necessarily achieve complete self-support. Congressional refusal to act on H.R. 1 casts serious doubt whether such support is forthcoming. The alternative is to supplement the public assistance system with the various programs that have been reviewed earlier. Under this approach welfare would retain the residual role assigned to it by the framers of the Social Security Act, containing the unresolved dilemmas of public assistance in a marginal program.

NOTES

1. U.S. Congress, House Committee on Ways and Means, *Report on H.R. 1, Social Security Amendments of 1971*, House Report 92–231, 92nd Cong., 1st sess. (Washington: Government Printing Office, 1971).
2. The President's Message on Welfare Reform, August 9, 1969.
3. U.S. Congress, House Committee on Ways and Means, *Social Security Amendments of 1967*, House Report No. 544, 90th Cong., 1st sess. (Washington: Government Printing Office, 1967), p. 96.
4. Edward Moscovitch, "Income Supplements—How High Should They Be?" *New England Economic Review* (January–February 1971): 4.
5. Footnote 1, p. 219.
6. U.S. Congress, Senate Committee on Finance, *Hearings on Family Assistance Act of 1970.* 91st Congress, 2nd Sess. (Washington: Government Printing Office, 1970).
7. U.S. Congress, Senate Committee on Finance, *Hearings on H.R. 163 11*, 91st Cong., 2nd Sess. (Washington: Government Printing Office, August 1970), Part 2, pp. 501–2.
8. U.S. Congress, Senate Committee on Finance, *Hearings on Social Security Amendments of 1971*, 92d Cong., 1st Sess. (Washington: Government Printing Office, 1971), p. 663.

Index

Library of Congress Cataloging in Publication Data

Levitan, Sar A
  Work and welfare go together.

  (Policy studies in employment and welfare, no. 13)
  Includes bibliographical references.
  I. Public welfare–United States. I. Rein, Martin, joint author. II. Marwick, David, joint author. III. Title.

HV95.L55   361.6'2'0973   72-3227
ISBN 0-8018-1420-0
ISBN 0-8018-1421-9 (pbk.)